SKILLS AND VALUES:
FEDERAL INCOME
TAXATION

SKILLS AND VALUES: FEDERAL INCOME TAXATION

Michelle L. Drumbl
Associate Clinical Professor of Law and Director, Tax Clinic
Washington & Lee University School of Law

Deborah S. Kearns
Assistant Clinical Professor; Director, Low Income Taxpayer Clinic
Albany Law School

 LexisNexis

Library of Congress Cataloging-in-Publication Data

Drumbl, Michelle L.
    Skills and values. Federal income taxation / Michelle L. Drumbl, Deborah S. Kearns.
        p. cm.
    ISBN 978-1-4224-7842-4 (soft cover)
    1. Income tax—Law and legislation—United States—Problems, exercises, etc. I. Kearns,
Deborah S. II. Title.
    KF6369.85.D78 2011
    343.7305′2—dc22

                                                                        2011013884

Editorial Offices
121 Chanlon Rd., New Providence, NJ 07974 (908) 464-6800
201 Mission St., San Francisco, CA 94105-1831 (415) 908-3200
www.lexisnexis.com

MATTHEW◆BENDER   (Pub.3303)

Table of Contents

Preface

To help students transition from the theoretical and academic study of law to the practice of law, legal educators are considering the reforms that were called for in *Best Practices for Legal Education*[1] and the Carnegie Foundation report on preparation for the legal profession.[2] These works, both released in 2007, identified ways in which legal education can better prepare students for practice. In the spirit of these recommendations and the ensuing conversations about legal education, *Skills and Values: Federal Income Taxation* seeks to help bridge the gap between traditional academic instruction and the practice of tax law by exposing students to the skills and ethical obligations essential to a tax lawyer.

Traditionally, law professors have taught tax law through cases and problems focusing on isolated Internal Revenue Code sections. This book takes an integrated approach, seeking to help students capture the "big picture" of the tax system through exercises in each chapter that present hypothetical client situations. Students will actively participate in the learning process through the use of online interactive exercises, practice-oriented research and fact investigation, client counseling and advocacy skills.

The exercises also provide students an opportunity to explore some of the ethical issues that arise frequently in tax practice. All lawyers are of course bound by the ethical rules in the jurisdiction in which they practice. Lawyers practicing before the Internal Revenue Service are also subject to the professional responsibility regulations promulgated by the Treasury Department in Circular 230. From the initial interview to the termination of a case, ethical obligations must be at the forefront of a tax lawyer's mind.

We have designed each chapter of the book to stand alone, so that students may undertake the subjects in any order. The book includes a number of integrated exercises that are not typically found in a primary casebook for a Federal Income Tax Course. We designed the chapters to be used as primary teaching materials at the option of the professor; if

---

[1] Roy Stuckey et al., Best Practices for Legal Education (2007).
[2] William Sullivan, et al., Educating Lawyers: Preparation for the Profession of Law (2007).

not assigned, the student can undertake the assignments independently as an introduction to new areas of tax. The online self-assessment materials, which include answers, practice tips, and illustrative tax forms, provide an opportunity for students to evaluate their understanding of federal income tax.

Acknowledgments

I would like to express my gratitude to the Frances Lewis Law Center at Washington and Lee University School of Law for its support of this project. I also wish to acknowledge and thank the following individuals: Sheri Hiter, for her research assistance and attention to detail as she read each of my draft chapters; my friend and former colleague at Chief Counsel, Nina Chowdhry, for her extensive comments on Chapter 14; and Ryan Au, for his input from the perspective of a law student in the earliest stages of the project. Additionally, I am grateful to Erica Knott for her work in helping oversee the Tax Clinic during 2009-2010, which allowed me to devote time and energy to this book.

Finally, I wish to thank my family. I could not have completed this project without the steadfast encouragement and support of my husband Mark and the patience of our two young sons, Paul and Luke.

Michelle L. Drumbl
Lexington, Virginia

This book would be incomplete without a proper acknowledgment of the individuals who provided tremendous support throughout the course of this project. First, I would like to thank my colleagues at Albany Law School's Law Clinic & Justice Center for their constant guidance, patience, and continued support and enthusiasm for this book. I would also like to extend my sincere gratitude to Professor Danshera Cords for her contribution to the policy and non-recognition exercises and to Associate Professor Rosemary Queenan for her feedback on several of the legal writing exercises. I also wish to acknowledge and thank the following students whose tireless research and assistance helped move this project forward: Guinevere Seaward for her meticulous research assistance in the beginning stages of this project; Melissa Perry for her research assistance during the intense writing phase of this book; and Kristin Camme for her help with the online portion of the project. Additionally, I am forever grateful for the administrative support of Rosetta Rawlins, the work-study support of Jennifer Charlton, and for the tireless efforts of Leslie Granger, Graduate Law Fellow. Their able assistance in the Tax Clinic allowed me to devote time to this book.

I am especially grateful for the love, devotion and patience of my husband Ken and our two beautiful young sons, Michael and Thomas.

Deborah S. Kearns
Albany, New York

Chapter 1

INTRODUCTION TO FEDERAL INCOME TAXATION

Whether you like it or not, your career path will undoubtedly intersect with the Internal Revenue Code (Code). You may not end up as a tax lawyer, but it is important to become familiar with the general principles and practical application of the Code to assist your clients in making sound personal and business decisions. At the very least, it is of critical importance to be able to spot tax issues and make informed decisions about the tax consequences of a proposed course of action. Knowledge of the policy considerations inherent in the Code, where to find the tax law and how to apply the law to a particular set of facts is crucial in making informed decisions.

Tax Policy

It is important to understand basic tax policy principles. There are any number of objectives that law makers may have in designing a tax system. The fundamental objective of any tax system is to raise revenue, however stimulation of the economy, the achievement of financial goals and the implementation of social policies are equally as important. In choosing among the varying objectives, certain tax policy evaluation standards are used: **equity**, **efficiency** and **simplicity**.

Tax equity includes both horizontal and vertical equity. Simply put, horizontal equity means that persons similarly situated should pay the same amount of tax. That is, individuals with similar incomes should be taxed the same. Vertical equity means that those with higher incomes should pay more to the government. Vertical equity is the justification for a progressive tax rate structure. **Tax efficiency** generally refers to the allocation of resources to their most productive use. Finally, **simplicity** means essentially what it says and can be applied in several ways when used as an evaluation standard. Simplicity can be used to assess the way a statute was drafted or the relative ease with which taxpayers can comply with the tax law.

Tax Rates

Another fundamental tax policy consideration relates to the tax rate structure. Income in the United States is taxed via a progressive income tax system.[1] A progressive tax system is designed to tax a larger percentage of income for individuals and businesses with larger incomes,

---

[1] IRC § 1.

1

while lowering the tax burden on those with lower incomes. Opinions vary widely on the fairness of a progressive tax system and what makes for a fair share of the tax burden in this country.

Tax Computation

The general income tax calculation is best understood with a visual of the calculation and a brief explanation of the component parts. The basic income tax calculation is as follows.

	Gross Income (§ 61)
Minus	Above-the-line deductions (§ 62)
Equals	Adjusted Gross Income (§ 62(a))
Minus	Standard or Itemized Deduction (§ 63)
Minus	Personal Exemption (§§ 151, 152)
Equals	Taxable Income (§ 63(a), (b))
Multiplied by	Tax (§ 1)
Plus	Alternative Minimum Tax (§ 55)
Less	Credits (§§ 21-53)
Equals	Tax or refund owed

As you are introduced to each section of the calculation throughout this course it is helpful to place the concepts in context. The Form 1040 (**see online materials**) follows the basic income tax calculation. The starting point is to determine the taxpayer's gross income. As set forth in more detail in Chapter 3, IRC § 61(a) defines gross income as "[e]xcept as otherwise provided in this subtitle, gross income means all income from whatever source derived, including (but not limited to) the following items."[2] Section 61 lists fifteen items of income specifically, which can be identified on the 1040, however, this list is not exhaustive. There are numerous cases in which the courts interpret gross income broadly.[3]

To arrive at **adjusted gross income**, the Code permits several above-the-line deductions from gross income. Above-the-line deductions reduce gross income and are typically more advantageous given that they are not subject to phase outs in IRC § 68 and percentage of income limitations in IRC § 67. IRC § 62 sets forth the deductions

---

[2] IRC § 61.
[3] *See, e.g.,* Commissioner v. Glenshaw Glass, 348 U.S. 426 (1955); Eisner v. Macomber, 252 U.S. 189 (1920); United States v. Kirby Lumber, 284 U.S. 1 (1931); Cesarini v. United States, 296 F. Supp. 3 (1969); Old Colony Trust Co. v. Commissioner, 279 U.S. 716 (1929); Philadelphia Park Amusement Co. v. United States, 126 F. Supp. 184 (1954).

permissible to arrive at adjusted gross income. Above-the-line deductions are found on lines 23 through 35 of the federal 1040 (**see form online**). The next deductions are called below-the-line deductions. As discussed in more detail in Chapter 11, these deductions are subject to income phase outs and percentage limitations and are rich with tax policy considerations. Below-the-line deductions, or itemized deductions, include deductions such as the charitable deduction (IRC § 170), the home mortgage interest deduction (IRC § 163(h)) and the property tax deduction (IRC § 164). The final step in arriving at **taxable income** is to deduct the personal exemption amount, which is available under IRC § 151 for the taxpayer, the taxpayer's spouse and the taxpayer's dependents.

Once the tax has been determined pursuant to the tax rate tables in IRC § 1 and the Alternative Minimum Tax (AMT) rates in IRC § 55, tax credits are applied. Unlike a deduction, a credit is a dollar for dollar decrease in tax. Most tax credits can only reduce the tax to zero and are therefore called **non-refundable credits**. Some credits, however, are **refundable** and can provide a significant financial benefit to low income taxpayers. Refundable credits are one way that the Code carries out social policies, and many low income households would be denied the benefits of the credits if they were not refundable. The exercises in this chapter are designed to highlight the distinctions between refundable and non-refundable credits and to elicit conversation on the policy implications inherent in both.

Research

Tax is a complex area of the law and one that changes frequently, so effective tax research is essential in resolving a tax issue. The primary source of federal tax law is the Internal Revenue Code of 1986, as amended. The scope of tax research is not just limited to the Code, however, but also to Treasury Regulations, IRS Revenue Rulings and Revenue Procedures, administrative pronouncements and judicial decisions. Other resources include the IRS' Market Segment Specialization Program (MSSP) and Industry Specialization Program (ISP), which focus on developing highly trained examiners for particular industries and market segments. In addition, legislative history will often give the reader insight into the Congressional intent in enacting a particular statute. It is important to keep in mind the different sources of primary and secondary authority in tax research. The following charts provide a quick reference to the most commonly encountered sources in tax research and the general hierarchy of authority for tax sources:

Authority	Guidance
Internal Revenue Code	Committee Reports
Regulations (Final and Temporary)	Proposed Regulations
Revenue Rulings & Revenue Proceedings	Cases Not Officially Published
Officially Published Cases	Private Letter Rulings and Determinations
	ISPs and MSSPs

Skills Involved: Problem solving, application of statutes, understanding tax forms, memo writing, policy analysis.

General Description of Exercises: Preparation of tax forms, calculations, memo writing.

Participants Needed: This is an individual exercise to be completed by one student.

Estimated Time Required: Exercise 1: 30 minutes; Exercise 2: 1 hour

Level of Difficulty (1-5):

Role in Exercises: Tax Associate, Tax Preparer, lawyer in a lobbying firm.

EXERCISE #1

Lisa and Samuel Mills are married, have two children (John, age 17 and Emily, age 15) and file a joint return for 2009. Their income and payments for the year are as follows:

Income

Lisa's wages	$40,000
Sam' wages	$45,000
Short term capital gains	$20,000

Payments

State income taxes	$ 3,500
Federal income taxes	$ 5,000
Property taxes	$ 5,500
Qualified home mortgage residence interest	$ 4,000
Charitable contributions	$ 500
Long term capital loss	$18,000

TASKS

1. Determine Lisa and Samuel's adjusted gross income (AGI) for 2009. To do this, prepare the Mills' 2009 Form 1040. (**Form 1040 online**)

2. Determine the total of their itemized deductions for 2009 and decide whether they should itemize for 2009.

3. Compare the Mills' tax return with the Davis family's tax return (**see online form**). Explain the significance of the difference in the child tax credit and the charitable and mortgage interest deductions.

EXERCISE #2

Congress has traditionally used the Code to promote social, economic, and political goals. One example is the deduction for mortgage interest on a qualified residence. The qualified home mortgage interest deduction is an exception to the general rule that denies a deduction for personal interest. The deduction has recently come under attack. You are a new attorney in a Washington, D.C., lobbying firm and have been asked by your boss to write a short memo on the impact of the National Commission on Fiscal Responsibility and Reform's (Commission) proposal to scale back the home mortgage interest deduction on your firm's client, the National Association of Realtors, Inc. (Association). The Commission's proposal would limit the mortgage interest deduction to exclude second residences, home equity loans, and mortgages over $500,000. A chief economist for the Association has predicted that limiting the mortgage interest deduction would bring on another recession.[4] The Association has vowed that they cannot support a "proposal that would chip away at the foundations of the real estate market."[5]

TASK

1. Prepare a short memo to your boss on the impact of the Commission's proposal on your client. Assume that it is fairly certain that the Commission's proposal will be adopted. To complete this exercise, the statute, legislative history and links to the National Commission on Fiscal Responsibility and Reform's proposal are online.

---

[4] http://www.housingwire.com/2010/11/10/obama-commission-considers-limits-to-mortgage-interest-tax-deductions
[5] *See id.*

REFERENCES — AVAILABLE IN ONLINE MATERIALS

Lisa and Samuel Mills Form 1040
Scott and Kelly Davis Form 1040
IRC § 163(h) Legislative History
IRC §§ 1, 21-53, 55, 61(a), 62, 63, 67, 68, 121, 151, 152,
161-170, 163(h), 164
Rev. Proc. 2008-66, Rev. Proc. 2009-50, Rev. Proc. 2010-25
Commissioner v. Glenshaw Glass, 348 U.S. 426 (1955)
Eisner v. Macomber, 252 U.S. 189 (1920)
United States v. Kirby Lumber, 284 U.S. 1 (1931)
Cesarini v. United States, 296 F. Supp. 3 (N.D. Ohio 1969)
Old Colony Trust Co. v. Commissioner, 279 U.S. 716 (1929)
Philadelphia Park Amusement Co. v. United States,
126 F. Supp. 184 (Ct. Cl. 1954)
IRS Form 1040 "U.S. Individual Income Tax Return"
IRS Pub. 17 "Your Federal Income Tax"
IRS Pub. 550 "Investment Income & Expenses"
IRS Pub. 936 "Home Mortgage Interest Deduction"
IRS Pub. 972 "Child Tax Credit"
Taxpayer Relief Act of 1997, Pub. L. No. 105-34
Economic Growth and Tax Relief Reconciliation Act of 2001
(EGTRRA), Pub. L. No. 107-16, 115 Stat. 38
http://www.housingwire.com/2010/11/10/obama-commission-
considers-limits-to-mortgage-interest-tax-deductions

A SELF STUDY ASSESSMENT IS AVAILABLE IN THE ONLINE MATERIALS

Chapter 2
TIMING PRINCIPLES

This chapter introduces a discussion of general income tax timing principles and the assignment of income and deductions to a particular tax year. An understanding of these concepts lays the foundation for the doctrinal concepts of income, deductions and credits and is important to understand as you parse through the material throughout the semester. The exercises in this chapter are designed to provide additional context to the complex timing principles in your text.

Accounting Period

The timing of income and deductions is dependent on two factors, the taxpayer's **accounting period** and **method of accounting**. The **accounting period** is determined by the way in which a taxpayer regularly computes income and keeps its books and can mean one of three time periods: (i) a calendar year; (ii) a fiscal year or (iii) a "short year" or fractional year.[1] A taxable year is adopted when a return is filed by the due date of the taxpayer's first taxable year. The most commonly used accounting periods are the **calendar year** (e.g., individuals) and the **fiscal year** (e.g., corporations). In most cases, taxable income is computed for twelve full calendar months. There are several other provisions in the Code that provide for less than twelve month tax years, however, for the purposes of this chapter, we will focus, on a twelve month year in the context of the calendar year and fiscal year accounting periods.

Method of Accounting

IRC § 446(a) provides that taxable income shall be computed under the method of accounting on the basis which the taxpayer regularly computes his income in keeping his books. Furthermore, the method must "clearly reflect income."[2] The two most common accounting methods used are the **cash method** and the **accrual method**.[3]

Cash Method

A **cash method** taxpayer reports income when it is actually received, in the form of cash, check[4] or property.[5] In addition, income will also be

---

[1] IRC § 7701(a)(23).
[2] IRC § 446(b).
[3] Treas. Reg. § 1.446-1.
[4] Charles F. Kahler v. Commissioner, 18 T.C. 31 (1952).
[5] Williams v. Commissioner, 28 T.C. 1000 (1957).

included in a cash method taxpayer's income under three income inclusion theories: (i) constructive receipt,[6] (ii) cash equivalent[7] and (iii) economic benefit.[8] If any one of these three theories apply, income may have to be reported faster than the actual receipt of cash or other property.

Although a cash method taxpayer is not usually taxed on items of income they have not actually received, there may be circumstances in which a one is taxed on an item they are deemed to have "**constructively received**."[9] The Treasury Regulations provide that constructive receipt of an item occurs when income is credited, set-apart, or otherwise made available to a taxpayer, unless the taxpayer's control of its receipt is subject to substantial limitations or restrictions.[10] If the taxpayer agrees to the deferral of the payment before the right to payment has been earned, the taxpayer will not recognize income until the payment is required to be made.[11] The rationale behind the constructive receipt rules is to prevent the arbitrary selection of the taxable year for recognizing certain income.[12]

Any obligation or promise to make future payments that qualifies as "**the equivalent of cash**" is taxable upon receipt as cash, as if the taxpayer had received cash instead of the obligation.[13] An obligation is a "cash equivalent" if: (1) the obligor is solvent; (2) the promise to pay is "unconditional and assignable, not subject to setoffs"; and (3) the obligation is of the kind normally transferrable to lenders or investors.[14]

Furthermore, gross income includes any **economic benefit** conferred upon a taxpayer to the extent that the benefit is capable of valuation.[15] For example, when an employer sets up a trust for an employee wherein there were no restrictions on the trust and the only duties of the trustee were to hold and invest the trust property for the benefit of the employee to be paid over time, such amounts will be included in gross income of the employee in the year the trust was funded. Setting up the trust conferred an economic benefit on the taxpayer on the year the trust was funded. IRC § 83 has codified the economic benefit doctrine in employee compensation cases and states that if property is transferred to a taxpayer in connection with the performance of services, the amount shall be included in gross income in the first taxable year in which the rights of the person are transferable or not subject to substantial risk of forfeiture.[16]

---

[6] *See* Treas. Reg. § 1.451-2(a).
[7] *See* Treas. Reg. § 1.61-2(d)(4).
[8] Sproull v. Commissioner, 16 T.C. 244, *aff'd*, 194 F.2d 541 (6th Cir. 1952).
[9] *See* Tras. Reg. § 1.451-2(a).
[10] *See id.*
[11] Robinson v. Commissioner, 44 T.C. 20 (1965).
[12] Hornung v. Commissioner, 47 T.C. 428 (1967).
[13] Cowden v. Commissioner, 289 F.2d 20, 24 (5th Cir. 1961).
[14] *Id.,* Treas. Reg. § 1.61-2(d)(4).
[15] *See supra* note 6.
[16] *See also* IRC § 409A.

Expenses

In general, under IRC § 461(a), a cash method taxpayer can only take a **deduction** for expenses actually paid during the taxable year. In the case of non-cash transactions such as checks, the deduction may be taken in the year the check is delivered, provided that the check is eventually paid and there are no restrictions on the time and manner of payment.[17] The IRS has also held that a credit card charge is a "cash equivalent," equating it with borrowing cash from the credit card company and thus, a deduction may be taken in the year of the charge.[18] Finally, although there is the doctrine of constructive *receipt*, there is no such doctrine for constructive *payment*.[19] Thus, a taxpayer cannot constructively take a deduction — the expense must actually be paid.

The general rule that taxpayers can take a deduction in the year an expense is paid is modified, however, by the capital expenditure rules in IRC § 263, which state in relevant part that "[n]o deduction shall be allowed for . . . [a]ny amount paid out for new buildings or for permanent improvements or betterments made to increase the value of any property or estate." Treasury has provided some relief to this non-deductibility rule by promulgating regulations under IRC § 263, which provide that a taxpayer is not required to capitalize an expense if the expense relates to the creation of an asset that does not have useful life that extends beyond the earlier of (i) 12 months after the first date on which the taxpayer realizes the right or benefit or (ii) the end of the taxable year following the taxable year in which the payment was made.[20] **[see Timing Explanations online].** The exception to the capitalization requirement under IRC § 263 was created for administrative convenience and does result in a mismatch of income and expenses in many cases.

Accrual Method

Timing of Income

An **accrual method** taxpayer reports **income** when **all events** have occurred that fix the right to receive the income and the amount of income can be determined with **reasonable accuracy**.[21] It is important to note that under this method, income is based on the *right* to receive payment and not on the actual receipt of money. In some cases, it is questionable whether the taxpayer will be able to collect for services rendered or sales made. In such cases, the right to receive is construed narrowly and the taxpayer may be left to include the amounts in income and then rely on the bad debt deductions provided by the Code when the debt is proved to be uncollectible.

---

[17] Rev. Rul. 54-465.
[18] Rev. Rul. 78-38.
[19] Vander Poel, Francis & Co., Inc. v. Commissioner, 8 T.C. 407 (1947).
[20] *See* Treas. Reg. § 1.263(a)-4(f)(8).
[21] *See* Treas. Reg. § 1.451-1(a)(1); *see also* Rev. Rul. 70-151.

One question that often arises with the accrual method of accounting is how to treat *pre-paid expenses*. Remember that the general rule under the accrual method of accounting is that the taxpayer reports income when all events have occurred to fix the right to income. The answer to whether or not a pre-payment will be included in income depends on the nature of the payment. Rev. Proc. 2004-34 lists the types of pre-payments that will and will not be included in gross income until accrued.

Timing of Deductions

Under IRC § 461(h), an accrual method taxpayer can take a deduction when all the events have occurred that establish the taxpayer's liability to pay, the amount can be determined with reasonable accuracy and economic performance has occurred. Revenue Ruling 2007-3 provides that all events have occurred to establish a liability when: (i) the event fixing the liability occurs or (ii) payment is due, whichever is earlier. Deductions under the accrual method are subject to the rules in IRC § 263 as with cash method taxpayers. Furthermore, contested liabilities are generally not deductible until the liability is determined.[22]

Finally, in addition to the requirements that the liability be fixed and able to be determined with reasonable accuracy, IRC § 461(h)(1) provides that "the all events test shall not be treated as met any earlier than when economic performance with respect to [the] item occurs." Economic performance in the case of services and property is deemed to have occurred when the services and property are provided or the use of property occurs. IRC § 461(h)(2). A deduction cannot be taken until the accrual method taxpayer has completed his or her end of the transaction.[23]

Forced Matching

The use of different accounting methods by two or more taxpayers involved in the same transaction may lead to tax consequences that do not fairly reflect the substance of the transaction. In that case, the IRS may make the taxpayers use a particular method to fairly reflect the substance of the transaction. IRC § 267 disallows losses, expenses, and interest deductions between related parties (see Chapter 12), and requires related taxpayers to match the receipt of income and deduction expenses. When it comes to related parties, the accrual based taxpayer will be placed on the cash method so there will be a deduction and inclusion at the same time.

---

[22] IRC § 461(f).
[23] IRC § 461(h)(3) provides a **recurring item exception** to the "economic performance" test if 4 requirements are met: (1) the "all events" test is met; (2) economic performance must actually occur with respect to an item within the shorter of (a) one year or (b) 8 ½ months after the close of the taxable year; (3) the item must be recurring in nature; and (4) either the item is not material or the deduction in an earlier year would better match the accrual of the income associated with the expense deduction.

Skills Involved: Problem solving, fact analysis, valuation,

General Description of Exercise: Counseling clients on timing issues. Relate doctrinal tax rules to client representation.

Participants Needed: This is an individual exercise to be completed by one student.

Estimated Time Required: Exercise 1, Task 1: 30 minutes; Task 2: 15 minutes; Exercise 2: 15 minutes

Level of Difficulty (1-5):

Role in Exercise: Attorney, tax preparer.

EXERCISE #1

Natalie Smith, a fifty-five year old corporate executive, has consulted with your firm to advise her on the tax consequences of a series of transactions entered into during the 2009 calendar year. Ms. Smith, a calendar year cash basis taxpayer, is employed by Widgets Inc., an accrual basis corporate taxpayer and has been working for Widgets Inc. for twenty-six years. She is concerned about her 2009 tax liability given that she sold 5,000 shares of Widgets, Inc. stock on February 16, 2009, for $128 per share, which she had purchased on May 22, 1998 for $58.25 per share. She is also scheduled to receive a significant year-end bonus ($100,000) on December 15, 2009 in addition to her $200,000 per year salary. Ms. Smith also sold GE stock at a significant loss to her brother, Steve, with the hopes of mitigating some of the gain related to the Widgets, Inc. stock sale gain.

Earlier this year, Ms. Smith decided to semi-retire and renegotiated an employment agreement to reflect this decision. According to the employment agreement, beginning January 1, 2010, Ms. Smith is to be paid an annual salary of $100,000 per year, payable in monthly installments on the 30th of each month for a period of three years. She also negotiated a reduced deferred compensation package that will defer 10% of her monthly compensation (as opposed to 15%) for the term of the agreement. This amount is credited to her account on her employer's books (not specifically set aside) with an adjustable interest rate tied to the short term applicable federal rate. The amounts credited to Ms. Smith under the deferred compensation arrangement will be payable to Ms. Smith upon the termination of her employment over a term of five years. The agreement is terminable at will by either Ms. Smith or by Widgets, Inc.

To celebrate her years of service and pending reduction in her corporate work schedule, Ms. Smith plans to take a tropical vacation beginning on December 14, 2009, and returning on January 2, 2010. She is traveling to a remote island in the south Pacific and will be unavailable by phone or email. Before she leaves for vacation, she would like estimates on her 2009 tax liability and to do some year-end tax planning. Ms. Smith is very concerned about her tax liability given her $200,000 salary, $100,000 bonus and stock sales. Prior to her meeting with you, she arranged a meeting with Widgets, Inc.'s human resources manager to request that her bonus and last month's salary be paid in 2010 given that she will be away on vacation. Widgets' standard practice is to issue checks to employees on the last business day of each month. Her employer has agreed to hold on to the checks until she returns from vacation in January 2010.

TASK #1. Consider the tax consequences and how you would advise Ms. Smith on the following transactions:

1) Would Ms. Smith be required to include any amounts in gross income upon the execution of the employment agreement?

2) When must Ms. Smith account for her 2009 salary? How much of her salary would be included in 2009 versus 2010? Consider whether the constructive receipt rules are implicated by this transaction.

3) Upon receipt of her first paycheck on January 30, 2010, Ms. Smith receives $7,500 (monthly salary less deferred compensation). How much of this income is required to be included in her income for this month? *See* Rev. Rul. 60-31.

TASK #2. Assume that Ms. Smith asks you to render her an opinion that the 2009 income is not includible on her 2009 Form 1040. Identify the ethical considerations involved in rendering advice to your client about the proper inclusion of the 2009 income and consider the consequences to you as the tax preparer and to the client in reporting the 2009 income in a subsequent year. [Consult Circular 230 and ABA Model Rules Online.]

EXERCISE #2

Tom Tenant, a cash method taxpayer, entered into a commercial lease with Lucy Landlord on January 3, 2010 to operate his coffee shop, Java Café. Both landlord and tenant are cash basis taxpayers. The terms of the lease provide for a five year term at a rate of $3,000 per month, payable in monthly installments on the 15th day of each month. Tom Tenant is responsible for the maintenance and upkeep of the property.

He is also required under the terms of the lease to keep adequate insurance on the property throughout the duration of the lease.

Tom Tenant retains practitioner Larry Lawyer to assist with the legal work related to Java Café. Specifically, a lawsuit has been brought against Java Café for a slip and fall on the property. Larry Lawyer is a cash basis taxpayer.

Based on these facts, complete the online quiz and consult the related self study.

REFERENCES — AVAILABLE IN ONLINE MATERIALS

Treasury Department Circular 230
American Bar Association's Model Rules of Professional Conduct,
ABA Model Rule 1.16
Online Charts Explaining Treas. Reg. 1.263-4(f)(8)
Exercise #2 — Online Quiz
IRC §§ 83, 162, 163, 212, 263, 267, 401(a)(5), 409A, 443(a)(2), § 446, 451(a), 461, 6694, 7701(23)
Treas. Reg. §§ 1.61-2(d)(4), 1.61-8(b), 1.263(a)-4(f)(8), 1.446-1, 1.451-1, 1.451-2(a), 1.461-1(a), 601.601(d)(2)
Rev. Rul. 54-465, 60-31, 70-151, 78-38, 2007-3
Rev. Proc. 2004-34, 2009-50
Kahler v. Commissioner, 18 T.C. 31 (1952)
Williams v. Commissioner, 28 T.C. 1000 (1957)
Sproull v. Commissioner, 16 T.C. 244, *aff'd*, 194 F.2d 541 (6th Cir. 1952)
Robinson v. Commissioner, 44 T.C. 20 (1965),
Hornung v. Commissioner, 47 T.C. 428 (1967)
Cowden v. Commissioner, 289 F.2d 20, 24 (5th Cir. 1961)
Vander Poel, Francis & Co., Inc. v. Commissioner, 8 T.C. 407 (1947)
Spiegel v. Commissioner, 12 T.C. 524 (1949)
IRS Form 8275
IRS Form 8275 Instructions

A SELF STUDY ASSESSMENT IS AVAILABLE IN THE ONLINE MATERIALS

Chapter 3

INTRODUCTION TO GROSS INCOME

As you are discovering in your study of federal income tax law, "gross income" is a very broad concept. IRC § 61 defines gross income as "all income from whatever source derived" and provides a non-exclusive list of 15 specific items of income. Law students are often surprised by what constitutes "income," and the case law — such famous cases as *Glenshaw Glass, Old Colony Trust,* and *Cesarini* — makes for great class discussion.

Beyond the rich and storied case law, you may also have a far more practical inquiry — how does the IRS enforce its rules with respect to some of the items that constitute income? If, for example, a taxpayer finds $1,000 in cash buried in his backyard (the so-called "treasure trove" hypothetical), what incentive does the taxpayer have to report this income, and how would the IRS know if the taxpayer did not? These are good questions and important ones to consider.

Voluntary Compliance and the Role of the Tax Practitioner

The starting point for the U.S. tax system is voluntary compliance — taxpayers are expected to file a timely return, report all items of income, and pay any balance due. In 2008, the IRS estimated a voluntary compliance rate of 84%.[1] As discussed in the next section, the IRS uses a variety of enforcement mechanisms to help promote voluntary compliance, to correct taxpayer mistakes and omissions, and to collect unpaid taxes.

Tax professionals play an important role. The IRS recently estimated that nearly 60% of taxpayers use a paid preparer to file their federal income tax return.[2] Tax practitioners and paid preparers are subject to various professional rules and regulations, and collectively they promote compliance and accuracy in the tax system. Anyone within the IRC § 7701(a)(36) definition of "tax return preparer" is subject to the Code's penalty provisions. For example, IRC § 6694 subjects a preparer to potential penalties for understating a taxpayer's liability on a return. Certain licensed professionals, including attorneys and accountants, are subject not only to the ethical rules of their profession, but also to the Treasury Department Circular No. 230 rules for practice before the

---

[1] *See* http://www.irs.gov/pub/newsroom/tax_gap_report_-final_version.pdf for this statistic and additional information on the "tax gap." The report states that, in 2005, the IRS estimated the net tax gap to be $290 billion.

[2] *See* IRS Publication 4832, December 2009, available at http://www.irs.gov/pub/irs-pdf/p4832.pdf.

IRS. Together, this framework of statutory, professional, and regulatory rules helps to promote and ensure integrity and accuracy in the tax system.

IRS Procedures for Enforcement

Despite a high rate of voluntary compliance and the role of tax professionals, the IRS estimates that a certain percentage of income goes unreported and unpaid annually. This shortfall is known as the "tax gap." The IRS relies on third-party information reporting as one important mechanism to promote accurate voluntary compliance and minimize the tax gap. Certain types of payors are required to send forms to the IRS reporting the amount of income paid to a specific recipient who is a U.S. taxpayer. The most common of these forms are W-2s and 1099s; generally the reporting party sends the form to the IRS and provides a copy to the taxpayer as well.[3]

The IRS compiles the forms it receives from third parties into a "Wage and Income Transcript" for individual taxpayers. If the information received by the IRS does not match the return submitted by the taxpayer, an automated process will generate a notice of underreported income to the taxpayer. The taxpayer will have an opportunity to agree or disagree within a specified time period. If the taxpayer does not respond, he or she will eventually receive a statutory notice of deficiency with a proposed assessment.

Underreporting income is one cause of the tax gap; nonfiling is another. If a taxpayer has not filed returns for one or more years, the IRS can use these third-party information returns to compile a proposed individual tax assessment. This automated process is called a "substitute for return" (SFR); the IRS will use the information it has received to calculate the gross income and then allow the taxpayer one personal exemption and the standard deduction based on a filing status of single or married filing separately. *See* IRC § 6020(b)(1). By failing to file a return, a taxpayer has not provided the IRS with any information about deductions, marital status, or dependents. Even when the IRS has received third party information returns showing likely deductions such as mortgage interest or student loan interest, these amounts are not included on an SFR. If the taxpayer does not respond to the proposed assessment letter, he will eventually receive a statutory notice of deficiency (also known as a "90-day letter").

A taxpayer may file a return at any time after it is due. If the IRS has assessed a liability under the SFR process, filing a return will likely reduce the liability if the taxpayer has a filing status other than single/married filing separately, is entitled to above-the-line or itemized

---

[3]   *See, e.g.*, IRC § 6041 *et seq.*

deductions, or can claim dependents. None of these items would have been reflected on the SFR. Unless the taxpayer can show that there would have been no liability at all (or that he or she would have been/is due a refund), a taxpayer will face penalties and interest for nonfiling/ filing late and for not paying the liability due.

It is important to understand the taxpayer's procedural options and respond to the communications from the IRS. If the taxpayer does not file a return or otherwise respond, the IRS will proceed with assessment and utilize its powerful collection efforts. A prompt resolution of a tax controversy is desirable, if possible.

The exercise that follows and the online materials will introduce you to some common IRS forms and notices, as well as the information that the IRS maintains for each taxpayer's account. It will also familiarize you with some introductory ethical issues and best practices.

Skills Involved: Application of ethical rules, problem-solving, fact gathering and analysis.

General Description of Exercise: Review the client's case file, which is available in the online materials. The case file includes: a Wage and Income Transcript, an Account Transcript, and a Statutory Notice of Deficiency. Also review the applicable law and ethical rules. Advise the client and prepare her Form 1040 both accurately and in her best interest.

Participants Needed: This is an individual exercise to be completed by one student.

Estimated Time Required: 30 minutes

Level of Difficulty (1-5):

Role in Exercise: You represent Barbara Baker in her controversy with the IRS.

EXERCISE

Barbara Baker calls your office in a panic, having just received a certified letter in the mail from the IRS. You instruct her to bring it over to your office right away, which she does. You determine that the letter is a statutory notice of deficiency and that Barbara has not yet missed her deadline to respond. You have the following short interview with Barbara:

You: "Ok, let's start from the beginning. This notice of deficiency relates to the tax year 2005. Did you file a tax return for 2005?'

Barbara: "Um. I think so. Or maybe not. Honestly, I don't really remember. I was having personal issues that year, and maybe I overlooked filing my return. I can't understand why they think that I owe so much money. I looked in my records at home, but the only thing I could find was this W-2."

You: "Ok. So was this the only job you had in 2005?"

Barbara: "Yes. No. Well, the only *real* job. I also tutor kids in math for a little extra spending cash. I think I did that in 2005. I'd have to check my diary."

You: "Ok. The first thing I'd like to do is contact the IRS to find out whether you filed a return. It appears from this letter that you did not, because the IRS has proposed a failure to file penalty. I also see the word 'non-filer' on their calculation page. It is likely that the IRS prepared a substitute for return, which is the basis for their proposed assessment. You can still file a return for 2005, and doing so could potentially reduce your liability for that year. We'll know more after I obtain your transcripts."

You have Barbara fill out IRS Form 2848, Power of Attorney, authorizing you to represent her before the IRS. Once this is processed, you will be able to obtain her wage and income transcript and her account transcript for the tax year 2005.

Review the online materials, and then counsel Barbara. Consider IRS Form 1040 as you determine whether the assessment proposed by the IRS is correct. What information (in the transcripts or unknown) is helpful to determine and/or to reduce Barbara's potential liability? As you prepare the return, what are some of the professional duties you need to keep in mind?

REFERENCES — AVAILABLE IN ONLINE MATERIALS

Barbara Baker's case file includes the following documents:
Statutory Notice of Deficiency
Account Transcript for Tax Year 2005
Wage and Income Transcript for Tax Year 2005
W-2 for Tax Year 2005
IRS Form 2848, Power of Attorney, for Barbara Baker

IRC §§ 61, 108, 163(h)(3), (4), 164
IRS Form 1040, Schedule A, Instructions, and Tax Table
for Tax Year 2005
Treasury Department Circular 230 §§ 10.22, 10.34, 10.51(a)(7)

A SELF STUDY ASSESSMENT IS AVAILABLE IN THE ONLINE MATERIALS

Chapter 4
DAMAGE AWARDS

Chapter 3 examined the breadth of the definition of "gross income," recalling the IRC § 61 description of "all income from whatever source derived" and its nonexclusive list of specific items of includible income. There are, however, Code provisions that explicitly exclude from the definition of "gross income" certain items that would otherwise be taxable. Part III of Subchapter B (IRC §§ 101–140) is entitled "Items Specifically Excluded from Gross Income." As a matter of statutory interpretation, the U.S. Supreme Court has repeatedly upheld the "sweeping scope" of IRC § 61's definition of gross income, while exclusions from income have been narrowly construed.[1]

IRC § 104(a)(2) is a commonly-invoked example of the Code explicitly providing for tax-free treatment of money received by a taxpayer. It provides that gross income does not include "the amount of any damages (other than punitive damages) received (whether by suit or agreement and whether as lump sums or as periodic payments) on account of personal physical injuries or physical sickness." The flush language of IRC § 104 adds the following: "For purposes of [IRC § 104(a)(2)], emotional distress shall not be treated as a physical injury or physical sickness. The preceding sentence shall not apply to an amount of damages not in excess of the amount paid for medical care (described in subparagraph (A) or (B) of IRC § 213(d)(1)) attributable to emotional distress."

Treasury Regulation § 1.104-1(c) clarifies that "'damages received (whether by suit or agreement)' means an amount received (other than workmen's compensation) through prosecution of a legal suit or action based upon tort or tort type rights, or through a settlement agreement entered into in lieu of such prosecution."

At first blush, IRC § 104(a)(2) might seem simple and broad, but in practice, its application as an exclusion is quite nuanced and limited. The characterization of the income is key to its tax treatment and is not necessarily straightforward. As the current version of the statute makes clear, punitive damages are includible in gross income. More subtle is the phrase "on account of personal physical injuries or physical sickness."

The word "physical" was not part of the original statute; it was added in a 1996 amendment[2] to limit the types of awards that can be

---

[1] *See* Commissioner v. Schleier, 515 U.S. 323, 327 (1995).
[2] Pub. L. No. 104-188, § 1605, 110 Stat. 1838. Prior to 1996, awards for nonphysical personal injuries could be excluded so long as they arose from a tort claim. See, for example, Gerard v. Commissioner (T.C. Memo 2003-320), applying pre-1996 law to exclude amounts received in a settlement for nonphysical personal injuries (emotional distress) arising from wrongful termination.

excluded from income. As quoted above, the statute as amended makes clear that emotional distress is not a type of physical injury or sickness. The 1996 legislative history specifies that "it is intended that the term emotional distress includes symptoms (e.g. insomnia, headaches, stomach disorders) which may result from such emotional distress."[3] The same legislative history also specifies that damages are to be determined by the *origin of the claim*, stating that "if an action has its origin in a physical injury or physical sickness, then all damages (other than punitive damages) that flow therefrom are treated as payments received on account of physical injury or physical sickness. . . ."[4]

Courts have frequently used a two-part test when determining whether the damages received are excludible from income—damages must be both 1) received on account of an action based upon tort or tort type rights; and 2) received on account of personal physical injuries.[5]

When advising a client as to the tax treatment of a settlement or damage award, there is a plethora of case law, administrative guidance, and legislative history to examine and consider.[6] In some instances, state law will play an important factor. For example, in applying the "tort or tort type rights" prong of the analysis, courts often look to state law to determine the nature of the claim. A lawyer must be able to advise his or her client on the tax consequences of a settlement offer or damage award; if this is beyond the expertise of the lawyer, the client should be referred to a tax advisor.

The importance of knowing when something is beyond one's expertise is underscored throughout the case law on the taxability of damage awards. When the IRS asserts a deficiency related to IRC § 104(a)(2), it often also asserts an accompanying 20% accuracy-related penalty under IRC § 6662 for a substantial understatement of income tax, if applicable. A taxpayer can avoid this penalty if under IRC § 6664(c), he can show there was "reasonable cause" for the understatement and that he "acted in good faith." In some cases, the taxpayer loses on the IRC § 104(a)(2) issue (i.e., the court holds that the income is includible) but wins on the § 6662 issue. The taxpayer may prevail in claiming relief from the underpayment/understatement penalty by showing that he relied, in good faith, on a professional tax return preparer (and had provided accurate information about the award to the preparer).[7]

---

[3]   H.R. Conf. Rep. No. 104-737, at 301, footnote 56 (1996).
[4]   H.R. Conf. Rep. No. 104-737, at 301 (1996).
[5]   *Schleier*, 515 U.S. at 337; the *Schleier* test predates the 1996 amendments that added the "physical" requirement.
[6]   For example, neither "physical injury" nor "emotional distress" is defined in the statute or in regulations. Taxpayers must look to these secondary sources for guidance on these terms.
[7]   *See* Espinoza v. Commissioner, T.C. Memo 2010-53 (award was partially taxable, but the taxpayer was not liable for the accuracy-related penalty because she had no education in tax law and relied upon the advice of her personal injury attorney); Longoria v. Commissioner, T.C. Memo 2009-162 (award was taxable, but taxpayer was not liable for the accuracy-related penalty because he relied on advice of a Certified Public Accountant).

One of the most interesting recent cases involving IRC § 104(a)(2) is *Murphy v. IRS*.[8] A 3-judge panel of the D.C. Circuit surprised the tax-practitioner community when it unanimously ruled in favor of Ms. Murphy, who had argued that the compensation she received for a non-physical personal injury was not income within the meaning of the Sixteenth Amendment because it was unrelated to lost wages or earnings. The panel concluded that § 104(a)(2) was "unconstitutional insofar as it permits the taxation of an award of damages for mental distress and loss of reputation."[9] The government then petitioned for a rehearing en banc and raised the new argument that even if the compensation was not "income" within the meaning of the Sixteenth Amendment, Congress still has the power to tax it under Article I, Section 8 of the Constitution. In light of the significance of these issues, the panel vacated its judgment and reheard the case. Upon rehearing,[10] the panel rejected Murphy's arguments and held that the compensation was "gross income within IRC § 61 that was not within the 104(a)(2) exception." While the *Murphy* rehearing opinion was consistent with settled law, the decisions opened up the possibility that IRC § 104(a)(2) is even less settled than it may have seemed.

The exercise that follows is intended to help you appreciate the complexity of the rules regarding damage awards and the fact-intensive nature of the analysis.

Skills Involved: Analysis of statute, case law, and administrative guidance.

General Description of Exercise: Analysis of tax consequences arising from a damage award settlement.

Participants Needed: This is an individual exercise.

Estimated Time Required: 30 Minutes

Level of Difficulty (1-5):

Role in Exercise: Client seeks a tax opinion regarding the tax treatment of the settlement award she accepted.

---

[8]   460 F.3d 79 (D.C. Cir. 2006), *vacated,* 2006 U.S. App. LEXIS 32293 (D.C. Cir. 2006).
[9]   *Id.* at 92.
[10] 493 F.3d 170 (D.C. Cir. 2007), *cert. denied,* 553 U.S. 1004 (2008).

EXERCISE

In January of Year 1, Arthur Employer, a musician, hired Claire Worker to be his personal assistant. Under their arrangement, Arthur called upon Claire to maintain a schedule for him and assist him with a variety of errands, both personal and work-related. On occasion, Arthur required Claire to travel with him. For the first several months, Arthur and Claire had a good working relationship. Over the next year, Arthur's behavior became increasingly inappropriate. He often made suggestive or lewd remarks to Claire. In February of Year 2, Arthur attempted to make sexual contact with Claire and touched her inappropriately. While this incident did not result in any physical harm to Claire, she began having stress-related migraine headaches and grinding her teeth in her sleep. In May of Year 2, while traveling together, Arthur again made sexual advances toward Claire. She fought him off and suffered bite marks and scratches in the encounter. Arthur later apologized; Claire, desperate for the steady income she received in this employment arrangement, agreed to continue working as his assistant. In July of Year 2, Arthur physically assaulted Claire, and Claire suffered swelling, bruising, and extreme pain. Claire spent several days at home recovering from the physical injuries, and before she could return to work, Arthur fired her. Claire sunk into a depression and did not have the will or the energy to look for a new job.

In November of Year 2, Claire hired an attorney. Claire brought a lawsuit against Arthur, asserting sexual harassment, wrongful termination, assault and battery, and intentional infliction of emotional distress. As permitted under her state's statutes, Claire sought damages including lost wages, medical expenses including psychological care, future medical expenses, compensatory damages for mental anguish and suffering, punitive damages, and attorney's fees.

In January of Year 3, Arthur's attorneys crafted a settlement agreement under which Arthur agreed to pay $45,000 to settle all of Claire's claims. The settlement agreement did not allocate the proceeds to any of the claims. In March of Year 3, Claire accepted and Arthur paid her the $45,000.

How should Claire report the $45,000 damage award she received under the settlement agreement? Must she include all or part of the award in her gross income for Year 3? As you consider the applicable law and reach a conclusion, you should also consider how Treasury Department Circular 230 §§ 10.33 and 10.35 might influence your response to Claire.

REFERENCES — AVAILABLE IN ONLINE MATERIALS

IRC §§ 61, 104, 105, 6662, 6664
Treasury Regulations §§ 1.6662-2, -4
IRS Publication 525, Taxable and Nontaxable Income
Commissioner v. Schleier, 515 U.S. 323 (1995)
Treasury Department Circular 230 § 10.33, Best Practices
for Tax Advisors
Treasury Department Circular 230 § 10.35, Requirements
for Covered Opinions
Private Letter Ruling 200041022

A SELF STUDY ASSESSMENT IS AVAILABLE IN THE ONLINE MATERIALS

Chapter 5
GIFTS AND INHERITANCES

Gifts and inheritances fit within the definition of gross income under IRC § 61(a), however IRC § 102 is an exclusionary rule and provides that property that passes to a beneficiary by gift, devise or inheritance is generally not included in gross income. Since gifts and inheritances are not included in gross income, it is particularly important to be able to distinguish gifts and bequests from compensation and other taxable receipts and to explain and apply the related basis rules of IRC §§ 1014 and 1015. It is also important to understand the limits of this exclusionary rule. For example, IRC § 102 does not exclude the income generated by property transferred by gift or inheritance,[1] nor does it excluded gifts and bequests of income from property.[2] The exercises and discussion in this chapter are designed to assess and refine your understanding of these commonly encountered concepts.

Donor Intent is Key

A threshold question in determining the income taxation of a gift or inheritance is whether the item received is truly a bequest or inheritance, or whether it is compensation or some other taxable item. In determining whether a gift or inheritance is exempt from gross income, the amounts must have been given with "detached and disinterested generosity."[3] **Donor intent** is the key to the application or non application of IRC § 102. The absence of a moral or legal obligation to pay does not mean the exchange of property is necessarily a gift, but if the payment is primarily from any moral or legal duty, or from the incentive of an anticipated benefit, it will not be considered a gift for tax purposes.[4]

Gifts and Bequests versus Compensation for Services

Where a bequest is made by contract to satisfy an obligation, it is taxed under § IRC 61, and is not excludable under § 102.[5] The true test used by the courts is whether the gift is a bona fide gift or simply a method of paying compensation.[6] Courts are suspicious of "gifts" made within the employer-employee relationship, given that a gift to an employee can provide incentive and motivation to an employee and

---

[1] IRC § 102(b)(1).
[2] IRC § 102(b)(2); Irwin v. Gavit, 268 U.S. 161 (1925)
[3] Commissioner v. Duberstein, 363 U.S. 278, 285 (1960).
[4] Bogardus v. Commissioner, 302 U.S. 34 (1937).
[5] Wolder v. Commissioner, 493 F.2d 608 (2d Cir. 1974).
[6] *Duberstein, supra* note 4.

other employees to work harder.[7] Given that it is difficult to discern the intent of an employer/donor in an employee gift transaction, Congress has created a blanket rule preventing gift treatment for employee gifts and bequests. Such amounts, will, therefore, be included in gross income of the employee.[8]

Income Tax Basis of Property Received by Gift

When property is acquired by gift, the donee of the gift acquires the transferor's adjusted basis in the property, which is commonly referred to as **carryover basis**.[9] This is relevant for income tax purposes because, when the donee of the gift later sells or transfers the asset, the gain or loss on the asset will depend on the original transferor's basis in the asset. Under IRC § 1015, there are two separate basis determinations that must be made — a gain basis and a loss basis.

The **gain basis** is calculated when the donee later sells the asset and the amount realized exceeds the basis of the asset.[10] The same rule applies to determine loss unless the donor's basis in the asset exceeds the fair market value at the time of the gift transfer. If the donor's basis exceeds the fair market value at the time of the gift transfer and the asset is later sold by the donee at a loss, the loss basis in the asset is the fair market value at the time of the gift transfer.[11] For purposes of the loss basis, the donee must keep track of the fair market value at the time the property was received. The purpose of this rule is to prevent the shifting of losses between taxpayers. The basis of property transferred between spouses incident to divorce is not subject to the basis rules of IRC § 1015, but rather is subject to the carryover basis rules as set forth in IRC § 1041 and is discussed in more detail in Chapter Eight.

Another consideration in determining the basis of an asset received by gift is whether or not gift tax was paid by the donor at the time of the transfer.[12] For gifts made after December 31, 1976, the donee's basis in the gift is increased by the gift tax paid attributable to the net appreciation in the property.[13]

Part-Gift Part-Sale

In some instances, a transaction may result in a **part-gift part-sale**. If property is transferred for less than adequate and full consideration in money or money's worth, a gift may result to the extent of the excess

---

[7]   Old Colony Trust v. Commissioner, 279 U.S. 716 (1929).
[8]   IRC § 102(c).
[9]   IRC § 1015(a).
[10]   IRC § 1001(a).
[11]   IRC § 1015, Treas. Reg. § 1.1015-1(a)(1).
[12]   IRC § 1015(d).
[13]   Treas. Reg. § 1.1015-5(c)(2).

of (1) the value of the property transferred over (2) the value of the consideration received.[14] An arm's length transaction between two unrelated parties that results in a bargain for one will generally not result in a part-gift part-sale.[15] The issue typically arises in bargain sales between related parties. A part-gift part-sale transaction may also cause a gift tax to be imposed, but for purposes of this Chapter, we will focus on the income tax consequences of sales between related individuals for less than fair market value.

The income tax consequences of a part-gift part-sale transaction are dependent, in part, on the fair market value of the property transferred.[16] For the transferor, gain is realized for income tax consequences to the extent that the amount realized exceeds the transferor's adjusted basis in the property.[17] There are no immediate income tax consequences to the transferee. In a part-gift part sale transaction, the basis of the property in the hands of the part-gift, part-sale transferee generally is the sum of: (1) the greater of: (a) the amount paid by the transferee for the property or (b) the transferor's adjusted basis for the property at the time of the transfer, **plus** (2) the § 1015(d) increase in basis for gift tax paid.

Income Tax Basis of Property Received by Bequest

When property is acquired by **gift or inheritance**, the recipient must determine the *basis* of the property for purposes of gains and losses when the asset is later sold or gifted. In general, IRC § 1014 provides that the basis of property in the hands of the person to whom the property is passed from a decedent shall be the **fair market value** of the property at the **date of the decedent's death**. For estate tax purposes, fair market value is the price at which the property would change hands between a willing buyer and a willing seller, neither being under any compulsion to buy or to sell and both having reasonable knowledge of relevant facts.[18]

Potential Basis Issues in 2010

The income tax basis rules for property received from decedent's dying in 2010 are a bit more complicated. Prior to December 17th, 2010, The Economic Growth and Tax Relief Reconciliation Act of 2001[19] (EGTRRA) had repealed the estate tax for decedent's dying in 2010 and replaced the estate tax and the corresponding step-up in basis rules under IRC § 1014 with the modified carryover basis rules of IRC § 1022. On December 17, 2010, however, President Obama signed the Tax Relief,

---

[14] IRC § 2512(b); Treas. Reg. 25.2512-8.
[15] Harris v. Commissioner, 61 T.C. 770 (1974).
[16] Treas. Reg. § 25.2512-1.
[17] Treas. Reg. § 1.1001-1(e).
[18] Treas. Reg. § 20.2031-1(b).
[19] Pub. L. No. 107-16, 115 Stat. 38 (June 7, 2001).

Unemployment Insurance Reauthorization, and Job Creation Act of 2010,[20] which repealed the carryover basis rules of IRC § 1022 and reinstated the estate tax and corresponding step-up in basis rules under IRC § 1014 for the tax years 2011 and 2012. Given that the estate tax was reinstated so late in the year, in 2010 the executor or personal representative has a choice: apply the estate tax *or* the modified carryover basis rules. The default rule for 2010 is that the estate tax regime will apply retroactively and the step-up in basis rules will apply to property received from a decedent dying in 2010. The executor or personal representative can, however, elect to have the modified carryover basis rules of IRC § 1022 instead of the estate tax and IRC § 1014, which has significant income tax consequences.

The carryover basis rules under IRC § 1022 provide that the income tax basis of an asset received from a decedent will be equal to the decedent's adjusted income tax basis in the decedent's property with a few modifications. If the modified carryover basis rules of IRC § 1022 apply, the basis of appreciated assets passing directly to a surviving spouse can be increased by $3,000,000, while the basis of assets passing to a non-spousal beneficiary can be increased by $1,300,000. The basis of the assets may not be increased to exceed the fair market value at the date of death. While this election is available for property received from decedents dying in 2010 only, it is important to keep these rules in mind when advising clients on the income tax consequences of inherited property that is subsequently sold or transferred.

Holding Period

For purposes of determining whether the gain or loss on the subsequent sale of a bequeathed asset is long-term or short-term, the donee will be deemed to have held the property for more than a year thereby qualifying the sale for long term gain treatment.[21] With respect to gifted assets, if the donee's basis is determined by reference to the donor's basis, the donee can tack the donor's holding period on to the donee's to determine whether the gain is long- or short-term.[22]

Skills Involved: Fact analysis, problem solving, application of statutes, understanding tax forms.

General Description of Exercises: The exercises in this chapter focus on the exclusionary rules of IRC § 102 and applying the doctrinal rules of IRC §§ 1014 & 1015 to fact patterns as they appear in practice.

---

[20] Pub. L. No. 111-312, 124 Stat. 3296 (December 17, 2010).
[21] *See* IRC § 1223(9).
[22] IRC § 1223(2).

Participants Needed: This is an individual exercise to be completed by one student.

Estimated Time Required: Task 1: 20 minutes; Task 2: 15 minutes

Level of Difficulty (1-5):

Role in Exercise: Trusts and Estates/Tax Lawyer

EXERCISE

Peggy Smith's father John Newberry died at the end of 2009 leaving Peggy, his only child, approximately $7 million in real estate, artwork, cash, marketable securities, life insurance and a qualified retirement plan. Your firm has represented Mr. Newberry for many years and has handled all of his income, estate and gift tax planning. You are named as the executor under Mr. Newberry's will as well as the trustee of the trust for Ms. Smith created under the will. Ms. Smith has come to you for advice on the income tax consequences of her inheritance and also wants to discuss the tax consequences of potential transactions that the family intends to enter into this year. Peggy Smith is the founder and CEO of Bedazzled, Inc., a successful marketing company in Dallas, Texas. She is married to William Smith and has two children, Alexis (23) and Brian (21).

In addition to the inheritance, Ms. Smith was the recipient of her father's generosity during his life. As part of his lifetime estate planning, each year Mr. Newberry would make a gift to Ms. Smith equal to the gift tax annual exclusion. This trend continued up until the year he died, however, in mid 2008 he began to grow concerned about his health and started to make several large gifts to Ms. Smith and her children. In July 2008, Mr. Newberry transferred a 3,000 square foot condominium in Telluride, Colorado that he purchased in 1995 for $250,000 to Ms. Smith. At the time of the gift, the condominium had a fair market value of $750,000. He also transferred his Adirondack chalet to Ms. Smith that he purchased in 2007 for $500,000 and which had a fair market value of $600,000 at the time of transfer. Finally, Mr. Newberry transferred 200 shares of IBM stock to each of his two grandchildren, Alexis and Brian, that he purchased on February 12, 2002 for $106.57 per share and transferred on March 18, 2009.

Ms. Smith sold the Telluride condominium to her son Brian in March 2010 for $400,000. At the time of the sale, the condominium had a fair market value of $800,000 based on comparable sales. Her daughter Alexis sold 100 shares of IBM stock on June 30, 2010.

TASK #1. Identify which items in the above fact pattern are includable in gross income. See online quiz. This task is designed to start you thinking about how the gift and inheritance transactions can arise in a family unit and how the transfers interrelate for income tax purposes.

TASK #2. Consider the following and provide any practical tips for the Newberry/Smith family based on your knowledge and understanding of the rules in IRC §§ 1014 and 1015:

1. Would the tax consequences of the sale of the Telluride condominium change if the condominium was sold to an unrelated individual? Would the basis be the same in the hands of an unrelated individual to whom the condo was sold? Would the sale of the Telluride condominium need to be reported to the IRS? If so, how would you advise Ms. Smith to report the sale of the Telluride condominium? Which forms would you use, when would they be due and what would they look like?

2. Assume that Alexis sold 100 shares of the IBM stock at a time when the stock was $81 per share. Counsel Alexis on the tax consequences of the sale.

REFERENCES — AVAILABLE IN ONLINE MATERIALS

Yahoo Finance
Big Charts
PowerPoint Quiz

IRC §§ 61(a), 102, 121(a), 691, 1001(a), 1012, 1014, 1015, 1016(a)(1), 1022, 1041, 1223(2), 1223(9), 2512(b)
Treas. Reg. §§ 1.1001-1(e), 1.1015-1(a)(1), 1.1015-5(c)(2), 20.2031-1(b), 20.2031-1(2)(b)(1), 25.2512-1, 25.2512-8
Commissioner v. Glenshaw Glass Co., 348 U.S. 426 (1955)
Irwin v. Gavit, 248 U.S. 161 (1925)
Commissioner v. Duberstein, 363 U.S. 278 (1960)
Bogardus v. Commissioner, 302 U.S. 34 (1937)
Wolder v. Commissioner, 493 F.2d 608 (2d Cir. 1974)
Merriam v. United States, 282 F. 85 (2d Cir. 1922)
Old Colony Trust v Commissioner, 279 U.S. 716 (1929)
Estate of Anderson v. Commissioner, 8 T.C. 706 (1947)
Harris v. Commissioner, 61 T.C. 770 (1974)

IRS Form 709 "United States Gift (and Generation-Skipping Transfer)
Tax Return"
IRS Inst 709 "Instruction for Form 709"
IRS Form 706 "United States Estate (and Generation-Skipping Transfer)
Tax Return"
IRS Inst 706 "Instructions for Form 706 United States Estate
(and Generation-Skipping Transfer) Tax Return"
IRS Form 1041, "US Income Tax Return for Trusts and Estates"
IRS Inst 1041 "Instructions for Form 1041 and Schedules
A, B, G, J, and K-1"
IRS Pub. 551 "Basis of Assets"
IRS Pub. 950 "Introduction to Estate and Gift Taxes"

**A SELF STUDY ASSESSMENT IS AVAILABLE IN THE
ONLINE MATERIALS**

Chapter 6
EMPLOYEE FRINGE BENEFITS

Fringe benefits are a crucial component to U.S. employee compensation packages.[1] Examples of the more common taxable fringe benefits include vacation and holiday pay, financial counseling (excluding retirement counseling)[2] and employer gifts and awards that do not qualify for the de minimis fringe benefit exception[3] or the employee achievement award exception.[4] There are also several non-taxable fringe benefits, which is where the value is often added in compensation packages.

The rationale for many of the statutory exclusions from gross income is that since the U.S. Government does not provide certain benefits (e.g., healthcare, disability and life insurance premiums), it is appropriate to encourage employers to do so. With respect to certain benefits such as the working condition fringe, no additional cost service and qualified employee discount fringe, the rationale for the exclusion is primarily administrative. In these cases, recordkeeping and valuation complexities drive the exclusion from gross income.

Despite the wide net cast by IRC § 1, section 132(a) specifically provides that:

[g]ross income shall not include any fringe benefit which qualifies as a —

(1) no-additional-cost service,

(2) qualified employee discount,

(3) working condition fringe,

(4) de minimis fringe,

(5) qualified transportation fringe,

(6) qualified moving expense reimbursement,

(7) qualified retirement planning services, or

(8) qualified military base realignment and closure fringe.

In addition to the fringe benefits enumerated in IRC § 132, employees may also exclude up to $50,000 per year for employer-provided

---

[1] IRC § 61(a)(1) states that "[e]xcept as otherwise provided in this subtitle, gross income means all items of income from whatever source, including (but not limited to) . . . [c]ompensation for services, including fees, commissions, fringe benefits, and similar items."

[2] Rev. Rul. 73-13; IRC § 212.

[3] IRC § 132(e)(1).

[4] IRC § 74.

group-term life insurance,[5] up to $5,255 per year for educational assistance programs,[6] up to $5,000 per year of dependent care assistance[7] and certain amounts per year for adoption expenses.[8] While it is impossible to cover all of the various fringe benefits in detail in this chapter, the exercises are designed to test and refine your understanding of some of the more commonly encountered fringe benefits.

The **no-additional-cost service** benefit enables an employee to receive a service provided by the employer without inclusion of the value of the service in gross income if a two part test is satisfied.[9] First, the service must be offered for sale to customers *in the same line of business* in which the taxpayer works, and second, the employer must incur no additional cost when the employee uses the service. Thus, U.S. Air or Delta Airlines can provide an employee with free airline tickets, but free hotel rooms in a city to which the airline flies are not a qualifying fringe benefit. The second part of the test requires that there be no additional cost, which means that the airline cannot lose a paying customer in order to accommodate the employee.

The **qualified employee discount** provides that certain discounts given to employees for *goods and services* sold to customers by the employer will not be included in gross income.[10] The first requirement is that the goods or services must be in the *same line of business*. For *goods*, the discount cannot exceed the gross profit percentage of the price at which the good is offered to customers. For *services*, the discount cannot exceed 20% of the price offered to customers. Amounts in excess of the gross profit percentage or 20% of the amount of the service offered to customers will be included in the employee's gross income.

The **working condition fringe benefit** excludes from income certain employer paid expenses that had the employee paid for the expenses him or herself, then the employee could have deducted or depreciated the value.[11] Examples of this benefit include CLE courses paid for by an attorney's firm, journal subscriptions related to employment, etc. Certain educational expenses that an employee could have deducted if paid for by the employee may also be excluded from gross income. Certain club dues are also excludable from gross income if they are use used for business purposes, properly substantiated and not treated as compensation by the employer.[12]

The **de minimis fringe benefit** exception is an example of a fringe benefit that is so small that it would make accounting for it

---

[5]   IRC § 79.
[6]   IRC § 127.
[7]   IRC § 129.
[8]   IRC § 137.
[9]   IRC § 132(b).
[10]   IRC § 132(c).
[11]   IRC § 132(d).
[12]   Treas. Reg. § 1.132-5(s)(3).

administratively impracticable or impossible.[13] The burden is on the employer to prove the administrative burden. Examples of this benefit include the occasional and infrequent personal use of the office copy machine,[14] meals and transportation allowances for occasional overtime work,[15] low value gifts for holidays and birthdays[16] and occasional theatre or sporting event tickets.[17]

Another popular fringe benefit is the **qualified transportation fringe**, which includes: (i) transportation on a "commuter highway vehicle," used predominantly for getting to and from work, (ii) transit pass, (iii) parking pass, provided it is on or near the employer's business premises and (iv) qualified bicycle expenses.[18] All of these exclusions are subject to dollar limitations. The term employee is defined narrowly under IRC § 132(f) and does not include partners, sole proprietors and independent contractors.[19]

Qualified **moving expense reimbursements** relating to employment are also excluded from income and are an expected component of many professional compensation packages.[20] To qualify for this exception, the employee must have been able to deduct these expenses under IRC § 217 if no reimbursement was received. Any amounts paid or reimbursed in excess of the amount the employee would be entitled to deduct under IRC § 217 will be included in gross income.

An employer can also pay for certain expenses that benefit employees and their family beyond the work environment. Under IRC § 132(m), there is a **qualified retirement planning services** benefit, whereby an employee can exclude any retirement planning advice they receive from their employer who is providing an employer managed plan. This exclusion is available for services related to the plan, but does not include greater financial planning services such as tax planning and legal advice. The non-discrimination rules apply to the retirement planning services benefit.

Meals or lodging furnished for the convenience of the employer under IRC § 119 are subject to a number of technical restrictions. The exclusion does not apply to any cash payments that are intended to be used for meals or lodging and thus, groceries, for example, are not meals and do not qualify. For a meal to qualify, it must be eaten on the *business premises of the employer* for the *convenience of the employer*. For lodging to be excluded from gross income, there are

---

[13] IRC § 132(e).
[14] Treas. Reg. § 1.132-6(e)(1).
[15] Treas. Reg. 1.132-6(d)(2)(i).
[16] Treas. Reg. § 1.132-6(e)(1).
[17] Id.
[18] IRC § 132(f).
[19] IRC §132(f)(5)(E).
[20] IRC § 132(g).

three conditions that must be met: (1) the lodging must be on the *business premises*, (2) the employee must be *required to accept the lodging as a condition of employment*,[21] and (3) the lodging must be provided for the *convenience of the employer*.

Finally, one last popular fringe benefit is employer provided access to **athletic facilities**.[22] Three conditions must be met for the value of such access to be excluded from the employee's gross income: (i) the facility must be located on the employer's premises, (ii) the facility must be operated by the employer and (iii) the facility must be used substantially by the employees, their spouses or dependent children.

Non-Discrimination Rules

The non-discrimination rules apply to many of the fringe benefits. These rules provide that if certain benefits are provided discriminatoily in favor of highly compensated employees, the benefits will be taxable to those highly compensated employees.[23] In sum, the non-discrimination rules **do not** apply to the following fringe benefits: (i) Working condition fringe benefit,[24] (ii) De minimis fringe benefit,[25] (iii) Qualified transportation fringe benefit,[26] (iv) Qualified moving expense[27] and (v) Athletic facilities.[28] The non-discrimination rules **do** apply to: (i) No-additional cost services,[29] (ii) Qualified employee discounts,[30] (iii) Exclusion for employer provided cafeterias and dining rooms,[31] and (iv) Qualified retirement planning services.[32]

Skills Involved: Fact analysis, problem solving, application of statutes and regulations.

General Description of Exercises: Exercise #1 is an online quiz and assessment designed to further refine your understanding of the fringe benefit rules and regulations. In Exercise #2, the student is independent counsel for a mid-sized company.

Participants Needed: This is an individual exercise to be completed by one student.

---

[21] *See* Herbert G. Hatt v. Commissioner, 28 T.C.M. 1194 (1969).
[22] IRC § 132(j)(4).
[23] *See* Treas. Regs. §§ 1.132-8(f)(1), 1.414(q)-1T.
[24] Treas. Reg. § 1.132-5(q).
[25] Treas. Reg. § 1.132-6(f).
[26] Treas. Reg. § 1.132-8(a)(3); IRC § 132(j).
[27] *Id.*
[28] *But see* IRC § 274(e)(4).
[29] Treas. Reg. §§ 1.132-2(a)(4), 1.132-8(a)(1).
[30] Treas. Reg. §§ 1.132-3(a)(6), 1.132-8(a)(1).
[31] Treas. Reg. §§ 1.132-3(a)(6), 1.132-8(a)(1).
[32] IRC § 132(m)(2).

Estimated Time Required: Exercise 1: 45 minutes; Exercise 2: Task 1: 45 minutes; Task 2: 30 minutes;

Level of Difficulty (1-5):

Role in Exercise: Exercise #1 = student. Exercise #2 = legal consultant.

EXERCISE #1

Test Your Knowledge — The **online quiz** is designed to test your understanding of the fringe benefit rules and to provide additional exposure to Treasury Regulations. The self-study provides the answers and links to the relevant Code sections and Treasury Regulations. References and links to the Code and Treasury Regulations are designed to demonstrate the nuanced application of the rules under IRC § 132 and to assist with federal tax research and statutory interpretation.

EXERCISE #2

The purpose of this exercise is to apply the fringe benefit discussion, laws and rules to situations as they may arise in practice. You have been hired as a legal consultant to NashSports, Inc. to help them devise pay and benefits packages for their employees.

Facts

NashSports, Inc. is a sports franchise management company in a mid-sized middle-American city, Nashvegas. The company is in a growth phase and is seeking to hire new employees in an effort to promote the city's NFL football team, the Rebels. NashSports, Inc., is hiring for a variety of positions and levels. It is important to them to attract and keep the most qualified individuals at all levels, however, as a mid-sized company, they cannot offer top salaries. While they cannot match the highest salaries, their mission is to foster loyalty and team spirit within their organization, and the company seeks to make the job more competitive by offering an attractive benefits package. They hire you as a legal consultant to help them devise pay and benefits packages for the following positions.

1) **Operations Manager in Charge of Marketing**: This is a high level management position that will be very visible to the public. This person will be the "public face" of the Rebels. He/she is expected to be at all games and team functions, orchestrate press releases and generate sponsorships.

2) **Operations Manager in Charge of Physical Operation**: This is a mid level management position that will be in charge of necessary improvements and maintenance of the stadium.

3) **Administrative staff**: There will be five positions open as support staff for management. These positions will include a variety of receptionist, phone, scheduling and office management duties.

4) **Stadium employees**: The corporation intends to hire 120 full-time employees for a variety of duties. These employees will perform basic cleaning and maintenance of the stadium, operate the food and team products vending sites during games, take tickets, and guide spectators to their seats.

Nashvegas is the state capital and the stadium sits in the downtown area, along the banks of the river that forms one boundary of the city. Although there are many residential areas in the city in general, the immediate vicinity of the stadium consists mainly of government office buildings and high rise corporate and banking offices. The few upscale condominium buildings in the area tend to have very high prices and small square footage due to demand. NashSports, Inc. maintains their corporate headquarters in one of the turn of the century, multiple use high rises, occupying floors seventeen through twenty, which is the top floor. The corporate offices do not require all four floors, but the company has held onto the extra space over the years because of the excellent location.

Due to the downtown location of the stadium, parking is quite limited. Thus, it will be difficult for employees to find parking spaces. There is a commuter rail line that has a stop two blocks from the stadium and a large parking area about five miles away on the other side of the river. Parking in the commuter lot and a round trip ticket on the train cost $12 per day. The commuter rail line management already runs special weekend schedules when the Rebels play in order to take advantage of the influx of spectators. They are willing to add additional early and late runs in order to accommodate NashSports employees.

NashSports owns a corporate jet which seats 12 and is used by the CEO and CFO to attend meetings, games, and to transport potential sponsors. NashSports also owns three customized coach buses that are used to transport the team.

The stadium is equipped with a state of the art physical conditioning facility which is utilized by the team members from 9:00 a.m. to 12:00 p.m. five days a week when the team is in training and not on the road playing. There is also a two bedroom apartment that has previously been used by the team's physical trainer. The current trainer has a family and owns his own home in a Nashvegas suburb so the apartment is currently empty.

Task #1 — Fringe Benefits Package: Design a potential fringe benefits package that NashSports, Inc. can offer its employees. In an effort to be competitive, the company wants to make sure it provides an attractive benefits package in the most tax and cost efficient manner. The company would not want to cause inadvertent tax consequences to its highly compensated employees. Once you have devised the package, make sure to indicate for the company which benefits will need to be included in income and therefore reported on a W-2, and which benefits are excluded from income under a fringe benefits exception.

Task #2 — Top Candidates: On Friday afternoon you receive a fax from CEO Bob Wilson giving you the details of the company's two top candidates for the Operations Manager in Charge of Marketing, Messrs. Willie Smith and Dunlap Quinn. Mr. Wilson, along with HR, wants to be able to properly advise the candidates of the tax consequences of the benefits package. Willie Smith is a 54-year-old male with a wife and three teenage children. He is currently the Operations Manager in Charge of Marketing for a major league baseball team. Dunlap Quinn is a former NFL quarterback who has been the acting Marketing Director for a West Coast NFL team for the past 4 years. He resides with his life-partner Daniel Lark.

Advise Mr. Wilson on the tax consequences of the benefits package for each candidate. Will the tax compensation of the packages be the same for both employees? Why or why not?

REFERENCES — AVAILABLE IN ONLINE MATERIALS

http://www.nytimes.com/2010/07/01/your-money/01benefits.html
Online Quiz
IRC §§ 61(a), 74, 79, 82, 102, 105, 106, 119, 127, 129, 132, 137, 162, 212, 217, 274(e)(4),
Defense of Marriage Act, P.L. 104-199 (1996)
Treas. Reg. §§ 1.61-21(b), 1.119-1(f), 1.132-1(b), 1.132-2, 1.132-3(a)(2)(ii), 1.132-4(a)(2), 1.132-5, 1.132-6, 1.132-8, 1.132-9(b), 1.414(q)-1T
Rev. Rul. 73-13, 73-529, 75-170, 78-392, 93-86
Rev. Proc. 2009-50, 2009-54
Hatt v. Commissioner, 28 T.C.M. 1194 (1969)
United States v. Correll, 389 U.S. 299 (1967)
IRS Publication 15-B "Employer's Guide to Fringe Benefits"
IRS Publication 521 "Moving Expenses"
IRS Publication 535 "Business Expenses"
IRS Publication 969 "Health Savings Accounts and Other Tax Favored Health Plans"

A SELF STUDY ASSESSMENT IS AVAILABLE IN THE ONLINE MATERIALS

Chapter 7

GAINS AND LOSSES FROM DEALINGS IN PROPERTY

Chapter 7 focuses on concepts of gains and losses from dealings in property, including the distinction and importance of the terms **realized** and **recognized** income, the characterization of gains and losses and the general non-deductibility of personal losses. These topics are typically taught in several different chapters throughout a federal income tax course book; however the concepts arise in unison in practice and are therefore discussed together in this chapter.

The starting point for the discussion of gains and losses from dealings in property is **basis**. In general, basis is the amount which a taxpayer has invested in property. Basis is initially determined upon the acquisition of property and may be adjusted as a consequence of subsequent events.[1] Under IRC § 1012, basis is generally the cost of the asset at the time of purchase. The cost basis can also include amounts that the taxpayer agrees to pay in the future. If property is instead exchanged for other property, then the fair market value of the property determines the cost basis of the taxpayer.[2] In addition to the cost basis, property acquired by gift or inheritance[3] and property acquired incident to divorce,[4] have basis implications.

The **adjusted basis** of property reflects subsequent events that cause an increase or decrease in the taxpayer's original basis. For example, IRC § 1016(a)(1) allows a taxpayer to increase basis in property by the amount spent on any *permanent* improvements or betterments; routine repairs and maintenance do not affect basis. In addition, IRC § 1016(a)(2) requires a taxpayer to decrease basis in property by the amount of any depreciation deductions.

Basis is often reported incorrectly due to poor recordkeeping, lapse of time and inaccurate valuations. A study conducted by the IRS in 2005 estimated that the federal government was losing an estimated $11 billion in annual tax revenues by the failure of investors to accurately report adjusted cost basis information. Starting in January 2011, brokerage firms must annually report cost basis and holding period information to customers and to the IRS in addition to gross proceeds

---

[1] IRC §§ 1012, 1016.
[2] Treas. Reg. § 1.1001-1(a). *See* Philadelphia Park Amusement Co. v. United States, 126 F. Supp. 184 (Ct. Cl. 1954).
[3] IRC §§ 1014, 1015; *see* discussion in Chapter 5.
[4] IRC § 1041(b); *see* discussion in Chapter 8.

from securities transactions.[5] Gross proceeds from the sales of stock are reported by brokers to the IRS on Form 1099-B.

Amount Realized

For income to be **realized**, there must be some measurable transaction. Pursuant to IRC § 1001(b), the amount realized equals the sum of any money received plus the fair market value of any other property received. Sales of property for cash and exchanges of property for other property are generally realization events. Included in "other property" is relief from indebtedness.[6] It is important to note that when the fair market value of property sold is *less* than the outstanding balance of the debt, the seller must still include the amount of the cancelled debt in the amount realized.[7] Some other realization events include involuntary conversion of property (because of damage, theft, bankruptcy, requisition or condemnation), transfer of appreciated property to satisfy a legal obligation or abandonment of property. As discussed in Chapter 5, a gift is not a realization event.

Recognition of Gain or Loss

Once income or loss is **realized**, it must be **recognized** to be subject to taxation or deducted from income. Not all realized gains and losses are recognized. While the general rule is that all gain and loss from the sale of property shall be recognized, there are several exceptions providing for deferral of recognition or exclusion including, but not limited to, the provisions of IRC § 121 relating to the sale of a principal residence, IRC § 1031 relating to like kind exchanges, IRC § 1033 relating to involuntary conversions, IRC § 453 relating to installment sales, IRC § 267 concerning sales among related parties and IRC § 1041 transfers between spouses. Many of these provisions are discussed in more detail in Chapters 8 and 12.

Taxation of Recognized Gains

Threshold questions that determine the taxation of income recognized from the sale of an asset are (i) the type of investment asset and (ii) the holding period. Whether the gain will be a capital gain subject to more favorable tax rates starts with a determination of whether a taxpayer is in possession of a **capital asset**. IRC § 1221 defines a capital asset in the negative and states that "the term 'capital asset' means property held by the taxpayer (whether or not connected with a trade or business), but does not include . . ." inventory, depreciable property

---

[5]   See new 1099 online for purchases and sales beginning in 2011, http:// www.irs.gov/pub/irs-dft/f1099b-dft.pdf.
[6]   *See* Crane v. Commissioner, 331 U.S. 1 (1947).
[7]   *See* Commissioner v. Tufts, 461 U.S. 300 (1983).

and real property used in a trade or business (but see IRC § 1231) and copyrights and similar property. Capital assets do include, for example, stocks, bonds, real estate not used for investment, jewelry, precious metals, fine art, and other collectibles.

Once a capital gain has been realized and is to be recognized on the taxpayer's income tax return, the relative tax rates are applied to the **"net gain."** IRC § 1(h). Net capital gain is defined in IRC § 1222(11) as "the excess of the net long-term capital gain for the taxable year over the short-term capital loss for such year." The process for netting gains and losses is as follows:

Step	Task
Step 1	Net short-term gains and losses
Step 2	Net long-term capital gains and losses
Step 3	Net shorts against net longs.
Possible Results	1. Net short-term gain in excess of net long-term loss. 2. Net long-term gain in excess of short-term loss. 3. Combination of net-short term gain and net long-term gain.

Capital gain income is often taxed at more favorable rates (as low as 0% in 2010). Throughout time there have been many changes to the capital gains tax rates; however the current rates on long-term capital gains are 15% and 0% (for tax years 2010 and 2011). Short-term capital gains are taxed at ordinary income tax rates. Whether a gain is short or long term depends on the holding period. Capital gain property held for one year or less is taxed at the short term rates while capital gain property held for more than one year is generally taxed at the more favorable long term capital gains tax rates.[8] One reason for the favorable long-term capital gain treatment is that the gain inherent in an asset often represents appreciation over a number of years and it is not reportable as income until it is realized. As a result, gain accruing over the years is bunched into one year for purposes of taxation. To mitigate this problem, Congress lowered the rate on capital gains.

Skills Involved: Fact analysis, problem solving, application of statutes, understanding tax forms.

---

[8] IRC §§ 1222(1), (3).

General Description of Exercise: Tax calculations, application of statutes, fact investigation.

Participants Needed: This is an individual exercise to be completed by one student.

Estimated Time Required: Task 1: 45 minutes; Task 2: 20 minutes

Level of Difficulty (1-5):

Role in Exercise: Tax Counsel

EXERCISE

Lauren Jones has retained your firm to provide assistance with her 2009 tax return. In addition to a 2009 Form W-2 reporting $75,000 in income, Lauren told you of the following transactions involving her personal assets, some of which were corroborated by 1099Bs filed with the Internal Revenue Service. Assume in each case, unless specifically told otherwise, that the asset is a capital asset and has never been used in, or in connection with, a business:

(1) She sold XYZ bonds that she bought on April 25, 2005, and sold on July 21, 2009. She bought the bonds for $25,000 and sold them for $28,000.

(2) She sold ABC stock on April 22, 2009 that she was given by her mother six months prior. The stock was bought as an investment by her mother, on March 18, 2007, for $80,000, and had a fair market value of $70,000 at the time of the gift. Lauren sold the stock to her friend Donna for $65,000.

(3) She sold for $40,000 jewelry on February 15, 2009 that she has owned for 15 years. She was given the jewelry by her husband, who had inherited it from his mother. At the time of the mother's death, the jewelry was worth $25,000 and at the time of the gift by her husband to Lauren the jewelry was worth $35,000.

(4) She sold LMN stock that she bought on October 30, 2008 on June 18, 2009. She paid $70,000 for the stock and sold it for $50,000.

(5) She sold her car, which she has owned for several years and used exclusively for recreational purposes. She bought the car for $35,000 and she sold it for $30,000.

In addition to her 2009 income, in the course of your meeting, Lauren disclosed that she thinks that she forgot to file her 2005 tax return. She was going through a rough time in her life during that year, and taxes were the last thing on her mind. She has very little tax information for that year. The only thing she remembers is that she sold several blocks of General Electric stock that she received from her father's estate when he died on January 23, 2004, and she may have sold some IBM stock. She also sold some gold coins that she purchased in the late 1990s, and she has some receipts for the purchase. There may have also been some income from some odd jobs, but that is all she remembers.

TASK #1: Consider the tax consequences of the above transactions and the impact on Lauren's 2009 tax liability.

a. What is the net gain or loss required to be reported on Lauren's 2009 Form 1040?

b. Where would Lauren report the above transactions? Prepare the appropriate schedule in preparation for a meeting with Lauren and explain the impact of the sales on her overall tax liability. What practical tips would you give Lauren going forward?

TASK #2: Advise Lauren on the unfiled prior tax return. Lauren has told you that she has very little tax information related to the year in question. Consider how you would go about obtaining W-2 and 1099 information. What information would you need from Lauren to obtain the tax information? How would you go about obtaining basis information for the stock sales? What additional information would you need?

REFERENCES — AVAILABLE IN ONLINE MATERIALS

Lauren Jones 2009 Tax Return, 2011 1099
Self Study
IRC §§ 1(h), 121, 165(c), 267, 453, 1001, 1012, 1014, 1015, 1016, 1031, 1033, 1041(b), 1221, 1222(11), 1231
Treas. Reg. 1.1001-1(a)
Philadelphia Park Amusement Co. v. United States,
126 F. Supp. 184 (Ct. Cl. 1954)
Likins-Foster Honolulu Corp. v. Commissioner,
417 F.2d 285 (10th Cir. 1969)
Crane v. Commissioner, 331 U.S. 1 (1947)
Commissioner v. Tufts, 461 U.S. 300 (1983)
Imprimis Investors LLC v. United States, 83 Fed. Cl. 46
(Fed. Cl. 2008)
IRS Form 709 "United States Gift (and Generation-Skipping Transfer)
Tax Return"
IRS Inst 709 "Instruction for Form 709"
IRS Form 1099-B

IRS Form 2848
IRS Publication 523
IRS Publication 550 — Investment Income and Expenses
(Including Capital Gains and Losses)
IRS Publication 544 — Sales and Other Dispositions of Assets

**A SELF STUDY ASSESSMENT IS AVAILABLE IN THE
ONLINE MATERIALS**

Chapter 8
ALIMONY AND DIVORCE

Oftentimes, life events have tax consequences — marriage, the birth of a child, and divorce are all events that impact one's tax liability. It is important to understand the tax treatment of transactions that might arise as a result of these life changes. Divorce provides an opportunity for tax counseling and planning as individuals negotiate a property agreement and settle other financial issues. If the parties negotiate carefully, they both might benefit from careful tax planning despite the fact that they are adversaries in the divorce.

One issue that arises is the treatment of **alimony**. IRC § 71 provides that alimony payments are income to the payee, while IRC § 215 allows the payor to claim a deduction for alimony payments unless the divorce or separation instrument designates that such payments are not taxable to the payee or deductible by the payor. The deduction is allowed as an above-the-line adjustment to gross income. See IRC § 62(a)(10). The ability to deduct alimony payments creates a tax-planning opportunity, and this will likely become a subject of careful negotiation between the parties. Alimony has a very specific definition — it must be a cash payment, must be made pursuant to a divorce or separation instrument, and must terminate at the death of the payee spouse. IRC § 71(f) provides that the excess "front-loading" of alimony payments will require adjustment by both payee and payor in the third post-separation year; this provision prevents the parties from structuring a property transfer as an alimony agreement.

In contrast to the treatment of alimony, IRC § 71(c) provides that payments of **child support** are excluded from the payee's income. Because child support payments are excluded from the payee's income, the Code does not provide a deduction for the payor. The terms used in an agreement are not necessarily binding on the IRS — for instance, a payment is not treated as alimony if it is set to be reduced when a child reaches a certain age, despite language in an agreement classifying the payment as alimony. *See* IRC § 71(c)(2). The regulations provide detailed guidance as to when the IRS will presume that an "alimony payment" is actually child support, in which case the deduction will not be allowed.[1]

Another tax planning opportunity arises if the divorcing couple has children. Claiming dependents as a **personal exemption** can be a valuable tax item. Which spouse should have the right to do so? The Code presumptively assigns this right to the custodial parent. However, IRC § 152(e) allows the custodial parent to release the claim to the

---

[1]   Treas. Reg. § 1.71-1T(c)

exemption, allowing the noncustodial spouse to claim the exemption. This will be another potential point of negotiation between the divorcing parties.

Property settlements raise yet another set of tax issues. Unlike alimony, a deduction is not available for property settlements. However, IRC § 1041 provides special nonrecognition rules for a transfer of assets between former spouses if the transfer is incident to a divorce. In that case, the transfer is nontaxable and is treated as a gift; the transferee spouse will take the adjusted basis of the transferor. In many cases, the marital home is the most valuable asset in the marital estate, and significant tax consequences can be associated with a sale of a marital residence. IRC § 121 provides for exclusion of gain from the sale of a principal residence when certain ownership and use conditions are met. In general, a single taxpayer can exclude up to $250,000 of gain on the sale, while a married couple filing jointly can exclude up to $500,000 of gain. IRC § 121(d)(3) provides special rules for property owned by divorcing spouses. The couple should bear this rule in mind as they structure their settlement and anticipate the future tax consequences.

The exercise in this chapter will help you to apply some of the federal income tax issues that are relevant to divorce and property division. It will help you develop skills in client counseling and appreciate the art of explaining tax as it relates to life decisions.

In performing the tasks, keep in mind that your primary role is to consider potential tax consequences, but that clients may have other non-tax considerations in mind as they structure their property settlement. An essential component of practicing law is to remember that the final decision always rests with the client and not the lawyer and to understand that there are often overriding considerations that outweigh the legal advice you offer.

Skills Involved: Fact analysis, problem-solving, application of statutes, understanding tax forms.

General Description of Exercise: Consider the ethical implications of representing the potential client; counsel client as to most favorable tax planning structure for his divorce and property agreement.

Participants Needed: This is an individual exercise to be completed by one student.

Estimated Time Required: Task 1: 15 minutes; Task 2: 25 minutes; Task 3: 20 minutes

Level of Difficulty (1-5):

Role in Exercise: Jason Williams has asked you to advise him about the tax consequences of his property settlement related to his upcoming divorce. You must decide whether you can represent him, and assuming so, how to advise him in light of the facts described below.

EXERCISE

Over the years, you have represented a married couple named Jason and Brenda Williams in various tax- and estate-planning matters. This morning you received an email from Jason with the news that he and Brenda have separated and plan to finalize their divorce soon. Jason would like you to represent him as he works out a property agreement with Brenda. He and Brenda have been married for 18 years and have two children together: Henry, age 15, and Stacy, age 13. Their only assets include the marital residence, two cars, and a joint bank account. Jason tells you that the separation has been an amicable process, and he wants to treat Brenda fairly; his goal is to structure the property division as favorably as possible from a tax-planning perspective.

Brenda will have custody of the children, who will live with her year-round. Jason will provide monthly financial support for the children until they reach the age of 21, and he will have full visitation rights. Jason will also pay Brenda alimony on a monthly basis. The precise amounts of child support and alimony are still being discussed.

Jason and Brenda own a home that they bought in 1999 for $100,000, which is now worth approximately $700,000. They put an addition on the home five years ago at a cost of approximately $50,000. They have owned and lived in their home together for over 10 years and are discussing whether to sell the home and split the proceeds; the alternative would be for Jason to transfer his interest to Brenda so that she can continue to live in the house with the children. Finally, Jason would like to claim the children as dependents for tax purposes, and Brenda is open to this idea as long as he pays her a sufficient amount of child support.

As Jason and Brenda agree on the specifics of their settlement, he would like your advice as to the tax consequences of each of the following: alimony, child support, and the sale of the home. He would like suggestions on how to structure his divorce in the most tax-efficient manner while balancing the non-tax needs of his family. He plans to rent an apartment; without the home mortgage interest deduction, he probably will not itemize deductions for the next several years.

TASK #1. Identify any ethical concerns that may arise from the past representation of Brenda.

TASK #2. Consider the most favorable structure for tax purposes and any practical tips for when Jason files his federal income tax return, focusing particularly on the following:

1) How would it impact Jason's tax liability if he structures his payments as alimony vs. child support? Are the payments both deductible? Must Jason itemize his return to benefit from the deduction(s)? Explain to Jason the significance of an "above-the-line" deduction vs. a "below-the-line" deduction. Based on your findings, what are your recommendations on how to structure the settlement in a tax-efficient manner?

2) Assuming that Brenda agrees to release her claim to the exemption for the children, advise Jason how to fill out Form 8332 and explain its significance. How much is this release worth to Jason?

TASK #3. Jason would like your advice on the tax consequences of the distribution of the marital home. Specifically, he has asked you to counsel him on the sale of the home. Jason would like you determine how much tax he would pay on the sale of the home and how to report the gain, if any, on his income tax return.

REFERENCES — AVAILABLE IN ONLINE MATERIALS

IRC §§ 71, 215, 1041, 121, 152
Schedule D, IRS Form 1040
IRS Form 8332, Release of Claim to Exemption for Child
by Custodial Parent
IRS Publication 504, Divorced or Separated Individuals
IRS Publication 523, Selling Your Home
ABA Model Rules of Professional Conduct Rule 1.6, Confidentiality
of Information
ABA Model Rules of Professional Conduct Rule 1.9, Duties to
Former Clients

A SELF STUDY ASSESSMENT IS AVAILABLE IN THE ONLINE MATERIALS

Chapter 9
INCOME PRODUCING ENTITIES

The Code recognizes three main types of income producing entities, partnerships, corporations and trusts and estates. In addition, sole proprietorships are a common form of business operations. Understanding the general comparative tax and non-tax consequences related to the different types of entities is important, because these issues cross over into many different practice areas. Exposure to these general rules is also important to see how the taxation of the various entities intersects with and impacts individual income tax planning. While an in-depth discussion of the taxation of the various income producing entities is beyond the scope of this book, the discussion and exercises in this chapter highlight the practical application of some of the rules that you may encounter in practice.

Sole Proprietorship

A sole proprietorship is the simplest form of business from an income tax perspective. As its name suggests, a sole proprietorship is owned by one person, and this form of business entity generally has few, if any, employees. The business owner typically utilizes a portion of his or her assets for business purposes and does not form a separate entity for the business. Sole proprietors will often do business under a separate business name, however, all income and expenses are recorded on the sole proprietor's Form 1040, Schedule C. As discussed in more detail in Chapter 10, one of the more common problems that sole proprietors face is documentation of income and expenses. Many small business owners are embroiled in the operations of the business, and recordkeeping and substantiation often go by the wayside. Proper recordkeeping is critical to the ultimate tax liability, given that the net business income or loss is reported on Line 12 of the 1040 and subject to federal income tax.

The net income from sole proprietor's income is also subject to self-employment tax. Self-employment tax is comprised of Social Security and Medicare tax. The self-employment tax rate on net earnings is 15.3% (12.4% Social Security tax plus 2.9% Medicare tax). The maximum net self employment income subject to the Social Security part of the self-employment tax is $106,800 in 2010. The Medicare portion of the tax is not capped.[1]

As with any form of business, there are advantages and disadvantages to a sole proprietorship. The main advantage of a sole proprietor-

---

[1] IRC §§ 1401, 1402, 164(f). Note that the Tax Relief, Unemployment Insurance Authorization and Job Creation Act of 2010, Pub. L. No. 111-312 (Dec. 17, 2010), reduced the withholding for Social Security tax for the employee portion from 6.27% to 4.2%.

ship is its simplicity. Other than a potential "doing business as" filing, there is no formal documentation necessary to organize a sole proprietorship. Given that there is typically one owner, the business ends when the proprietor dies, which also adds to the potential level of simplicity, but also has its disadvantages. From a non-tax perspective, the major disadvantage of a sole proprietorship is that there is unlimited liability to third parties for lawsuits. A creditor of the business can reach the owner's personal assets.

Partnership

A partnership is an association of two or more persons who organize to operate a business at a profit.[2] Partnerships are not subject to federal income tax at the partnership level, but must nevertheless file tax returns (Form 1065) showing net income or loss for a taxable year. Subchapter K of the IRC (§§ 701 through 761) governs the taxation of partnerships and is one of the most complicated subchapters in the Code. The partnership is considered a "conduit" through which partnership income or loss flows through to the partners, who are then taxed on their share of partnership's income (or receive deductions for any partnership loss).[3] At the end of the taxable year, the partnership will issue a Form K-1 to the individual partner who will then report the income and deductions on his or her Form 1040, Schedule E and other appropriate schedules. A partnership is generally required to conform its taxable year to that of its partners, which means that most partnerships operate on a calendar year.[4]

For state law purposes, a partnership is recognized as an entity that is separate from its members.[5] Unlike the business assets of a sole proprietorship, the assets of the partnership are treated as belonging to a business and are separate and distinct from the individual assets of its members. There are no limitations on the number of partners in a partnership and, in general, entities and individuals can be partners.[6]

There are two types of partnerships, general and limited liability. A general partnership, much like a sole proprietorship, does not provide protection from creditor claims, which is its main disadvantage.[7] Limited liability partnerships, on the other hand, provide certain limited partners with protection from liability up to the partner's investment in the partnership.[8] The advent of Limited Liability Corporations

---

[2] UPA § 1; Uniform Partnership Act (1997) http://www.law.upenn.edu/bll/archives/ulc/fnact99/1990s/upa97fa.pdf; IRC § 761(a), Treas. Reg. §§ 1.761-1(a), 301.7701-2(a).
[3] Treas. Reg. § 1.702-1(a)(8)(iii).
[4] IRC § 706(b).
[5] U.P.A. § 201 (1997).
[6] See IRC § 761(b); Treas. Reg. §§ 1.761-1(b), 301.7701-3.
[7] U.P.A. § 307 (1997).
[8] Treas. Reg. § 301.7701-3(b)(ii).

(LLCs) has significantly decreased the use of the partnership form of doing business in many instances.

Limited Liability Corporation

Limited Liability Corporations are a relatively recent creature of state law and have come to be the entity of choice for many business owners. For tax purposes, the IRS treats the LLC as an eligible entity under the "check-the-box" rules.[9] This means that the LLC has the flexibility to be classified as either a partnership,[10] an association taxable as a corporation,[11] or a disregarded entity.[12] If the LLC is treated as a partnership under the check-the-box rules because it has more than one member, the LLC provides a combination of limited liability, the flow-through of tax items, and the absence of S corporation restrictions on ownership and other attributes.

An LLC files a return based on the type of entity it chose to be for tax purposes. A single member LLC is taxed as a sole proprietorship, and all income and deductions related to the LLC will be reported on the member's Form 1040, Schedule C.[13] If the LLC chooses to be taxed as a partnership, the LLC would file a Form 1065. In addition to income tax, unlike S corporations, the members of an LLC are subject to self-employment tax on earnings. Many of the limitations placed on S corporations do not apply to LLCs, however. For example, there are fewer restrictions on who can be a member of an LLC and how profit and loss is allocated among the members of an LLC. Prior to the enactment of LLC statutes, the S corporation was more commonly used.

S Corporation

An S corporation is a small business corporation that for non-tax purposes operates as a regular corporation.[14] For tax purposes, an S corporation is treated similar to a partnership and acts as a conduit, therefore all items of income, loss, deductions and credits pass through the entity to the individual shareholders. The taxation of S corporations is governed by Subchapter S of the Code (IRC §§ 1361 through 1380). The income, loss, deduction and credits are includable on the individual shareholder's Form 1040 in proportion to the shareholder's interest in the entity.

An S corporation is a calendar year taxpayer and is required to file a Form 1120S by the 15th day of the third month following the end of the

---

[9]   Treas. Reg. § 301.7701-3(c).
[10]   Treas. Reg. § 301.7701-2(c).
[11]   Treas. Reg. § 301.7701-2(b).
[12]   Treas. Reg. § 301.7701-3(a).
[13]   Treas. Reg. § 301.7701-3(c).
[14]   IRC § 1361.

entity's tax year (March 15th). The shareholder's pro rata share of the income from the entity is reported to the shareholder on a Form K-1, prepared with the Form 1120S and distributed to the shareholder.[15] To qualify as an S corporation, the corporation must be a domestic corporation and meet the following requirements:

1. 100 shareholders or less;

2. Shareholders must be individuals, estates and certain trusts;

3. Shareholders must not be nonresident aliens; and

4. The corporation cannot issue more than one class of stock.

To qualify as an S corporation, the corporation also must make an election by filing Form 2553, Election by a Small Business Corporation with the IRS that is signed by all of the shareholders.[16] IRC § 1361(a)(2). The election must be filed with the IRS by the 15th day of the third month of the taxable year in which the election is to take effect.[17] If this date is missed, the election will take effect at the beginning of the next taxable year. IRC § 1362(b). If an election is not made, the default rule is that the entity will be taxed as a C corporation. Shareholders are subject to self-employment tax on their reasonable salary, however, any income not classified as salary will not be subject to self-employment tax.[18]

For non-tax purposes, an S corporation operates much like a C corporation. The main non-tax advantage of a corporation is limited liability of shareholders. Unlike a sole proprietor or general partnership, the liability of the shareholders is limited to the shareholder's investment in the entity. The shareholder's personal assets are protected from creditors of the corporation. Other advantages of a corporation include ease of transferability (subject to restrictions in a buy-sell agreement) and continuity of corporate life upon the death of a shareholder. There are several disadvantages to this corporate form including the taxation of fringe benefits for a 2% shareholder, restrictive buy-sell agreements, restrictions on the type and amount of shareholders and classes of shares and the administrative and cost considerations in incorporating the entity and operating the corporation.[19]

C Corporation

C corporations are governed by Subchapter C of the Code (IRC §§ 301 through 385) and are a separate legal entity from their owners for tax and non-tax purposes. C corporations are typically large publicly

---

[15] IRC §§ 1363(a), 1374, 1375.
[16] IRC § 1361(a)(2).
[17] *Id.*
[18] IRC § 1402(a)(2); Ruckman v. Commissioner, T.C. Memo 1998-83.
[19] IRC §§ 1372(a)(1), (a)(2).

traded corporations with more than 100 shareholders. For tax purposes, they are subject to double taxation: the corporation is taxed on the income of the corporation[20] and the shareholders are taxed on any income paid out to the shareholders in the form of dividends or compensation for services.[21] The C corporation does not get a deduction for dividends paid to shareholders, and the shareholders cannot deduct corporate losses on an individual Form 1040.

C corporations file a Form 1120. In general, corporate returns are due the 15th day of the third month after the end of the corporation's tax year. Unlike S corporations and partnerships, C corporations can elect to use a fiscal year.[22] The income from C corporations intersects with individual income tax planning, in that when a corporation pays out dividends, it will issue a 1099-DIV to the individual taxpayer.[23] Dividend income from the 1099-Div is reported on Schedule B of the taxpayer's Form 1040.

The main advantage to using a corporate form as an entity is limited liability. In addition, corporations have a perpetual life and centralized statutory management. Like S corporations, shareholder exposure to claims against the corporation is limited to the shareholder's investment in the entity. Corporations are creatures of state law, and they are costly and administratively complex.[24]

Trusts and Estates

Taxable income of trusts or estates is taxed to the entity or to its beneficiaries to the extent that each has received the income of the entity, which makes them a hybrid of sorts.[25] The taxation of trusts and estates is governed by Subchapter J of the Internal Revenue Code (IRC §§ 641-692) and provides that these entities are generally taxed in the same manner as an individual.[26] The tax rates for trusts and estates are significantly compressed,[27] therefore proper income tax planning is critical. Trusts, unlike estates, are required to use a calendar year for tax purposes.[28]

There are several points at which estates and trusts intersect with individual income taxation. For estates, upon the death of a taxpayer, a final Form 1040 must be filed by the executor, administrator or personal

---

[20] IRC § 11.
[21] IRC §§ 301, 306.
[22] IRC § 441, Treas. Reg. § 1.441-1(c).
[23] IRC §§ 301, 306.
[24] IRC §§ 195 and 248 provide some relief for the start-up and organizational costs.
[25] When using the term income in the Subchapter J context without a modifier (e.g., taxable income, gross income), the Code is referring to accounting income. Treas. Reg. 1.643(b)-1. Accounting income is based on the controlling document or state law, but typically does not include capital gains, which means that capital gain income generated by a trust or estate is taxed at the entity level.
[26] IRC § 641(b).
[27] IRC § 1.
[28] IRC § 644.

representative of the estate by April 15th of the year following the tax-payer's death.[29] Upon a taxpayer's death, a new taxpaying entity is also created — the estate. The estate, like a trust, reports all income and expenses of the entity on a Form 1041, which is due on the 15th day of the fourth month following the end of the entity's fiscal year.[30] For trusts, the terms of the trust govern the taxation of the entity, however any income paid to a beneficiary will also be included on the beneficiary's Form 1040. The ability of an estate to elect a fiscal year presents planning opportunities for the beneficiaries and trusts that are recipients of estate income. For example:

> Example: Decedent died on February 15, 2009. The executor can elect a long or short fiscal year, or may elect a calendar year. If the estate elects a fiscal year ending Jan. 31, 2010, all distributions made to the beneficiary are considered to be made on the last day of the estate's fiscal year. Thus, if the estate distributes income to the beneficiary on Dec. 5, 2009, the beneficiary is not deemed to receive the income until 2010 when the estate's fiscal year closes. In that case, the beneficiary will not be liable for income tax on this distribution until April 18, 2011, when the beneficiaries Form 1040 for 2010 is due. If instead, the same estate were on a calendar year and made the distribution on December 5, 2009, the beneficiary would be required to include the income on his or her Form 1040 due on April 15, 2010, a full year earlier.

Distributions from a trust or an estate result in income to the beneficiary and are reported to the beneficiary on a Form K-1. The estate or trust is entitled to a corresponding distribution deduction equal to the beneficiary's required income inclusion.[31] The deduction and corresponding income inclusion are limited to the entity's distributable net income (DNI).[32] The DNI concept places an upper limit on the amount of the distribution includable in the beneficiary's income and determines the character of the distribution as well.

Finally, when the creator of a trust retains too much control over the trust, he or she will be deemed to be the owner of the trust assets for income tax purposes. IRC §§ 673-677 and 679 set forth the circumstances under which a trust will be deemed a grantor trust. The grantor trust rules were originally meant to discourage trusts from shifting income to lower-bracket taxpayers, however, the compressed tax brackets applicable to trusts and estates has in large part eliminated this concern.

---

[29] IRC § 6012(b)(1).
[30] Treas. Reg. § 1.441-1T(b)(2).
[31] IRC §§ 651, 652, 661, 662.
[32] IRC § 643.

General Description of Exercises: The exercises in this chapter are designed to illustrate how the different forms of business entities intersect with individual income tax planning.

Participants Needed: Individual exercises to be completed by one student.

Estimated Time Required: Exercise #1: 90 minutes; Exercise #2: 60 minutes

Level of Difficulty (1-5):

Role in Exercise: Associate in law firm.

EXERCISE #1

Stuart Johnson, age 56, and Marge Johnson, age 54, have been married for thirty years. They have three natural children, David, age 26; Lisa, age 24; and Donald, age 18. David is divorced with no children and has filed for bankruptcy twice, so far, in his life. Lisa is married and has two children — Steven age 4, and Joan, age 2. Donald is unmarried and still lives with his parents.

Stuart Johnson and his wife come to your firm to discuss their estate planning after Stuart attended a bank-sponsored lecture on estate planning. After discussing the matter with Partner X of your firm, Mr. Johnson is willing to create a trust for Marge during her life, with the remainder of the trust passing to his three children in further trust. If Marge does not survive Stuart, the residuary estate will pass to Stuart's lineal descendants. Stuart is content to have Marge remain as the primary beneficiary of the profit sharing plan benefits. Mr. Johnson executed his will on February 1, 2009, and died three months later on May 1, 2009. **(see will online)**. At his death, Mr. Johnson had the following assets.

Cash	$ 35,000
Interests in various Mutual Funds	950,000
Shares in XYZ stock	85,000
Family Residence	75,000
Life Insurance	400,000

Profit Sharing Plan	600,000
Joint Account	10,000
	$2,155,000

As the executrix of the estate, Marge has contacted Partner X to help administer her late husband's estate. In addition to asset transfers, Marge has sought advice to determine what if anything needs to be considered from an income tax perspective. She is also a trustee of the trust created for her benefit and would like advice on the income tax implications of the trust (**see trust in will online**). Specifically, Marge has sought advice on the following:

1. Does she need to file a 2009 Form 1040 for her late husband? If so, what should be included on the return?

2. Marge would like your advice on the how to structure the estate for income tax purposes. Specifically, she was told by her CPA friend that there was some income tax planning that she could do through the choice of a tax year for the estate. She also would like to know what, if any, income tax forms would be due by the estate.

3. Finally, Marge would like to know how the income generated by the assets in the trust will impact her tax return.

Marge is coming in to meet with Partner X next week. Partner X is tied up in meetings this week and will not have time to prepare for the meeting. He has asked you to prepare a written memo to the file to address each of the three income tax concerns that Marge has raised.

EXERCISE #2

Samuel Mills (from Chapter 1) has approached you to help him decide how he and should organize his consulting business. At this time, he is one of four consultants that intend to go into business together, and he has independently sought your advice. Mr. Mills is particularly concerned about the tax consequences of his choice of entity, the cost and complexity of administration, and he wants to make sure his personal assets are protected from the liabilities of the business. He anticipates losses in the early years of the business and hopes to bring in investors as the business grows.

1. In preparation for your counseling meeting with him, he would like a brief summary, in writing, of which entity or entities would be most appropriate for his business. Prepare a letter to Mr. Mills explaining which entities you think would best achieve his goals.

2. Assume that the business is organized as an LLC. The LLC issues a K-1 (**see online**) to Mr. Mills at the end of the year with $5,000 in ordinary business losses reported on line 1 and $200 in interest income reported on line 5. Using the return that you prepared for Mr. Mills in Chapter 1, how would the income and losses of the business impact his return? Where should the income reported on the K-1 be reported on Mr. and Mrs. Mills' Form 1040?

3. Assume further that Mr. and Mrs. Mills bought 10 shares of XYZ stock that have generated qualified dividends during the tax year. How would the dividends be reported and impact their return?

REFERENCES — AVAILABLE IN ONLINE MATERIALS

Uniform Partnership Act http://www.law.upenn.edu/bll/archives/ulc/fnact99/1990s/upa97fa.pdf
Uniform Principal and Income Act http://www.law.upenn.edu/bll/archives/ulc/upaia/2000final.pdf
Treasury Department Circular 230
ABA Model Rules of Professional Conduct, Rule 1.2, Rule 1.4
Mills 2009 Income Tax Return
Mills Form 1065 K-1
Mills 1099-Div
IRC §§ 1, 11, 164(f), 183, 195, 248, 301 – 385, 301, 306, 441, 641, 643, 644, 651, 652, 661, 662, 673 – 677, 679, 691, 641 – 692, 701 – 761, 703(a), 761(a), 1361 – 1380, 1361, 1362, 1363(a), 1372(a); 1374; 1375, 1401, 1402, 6012(b)(1),
Pub. L. 109-222, 120 Stat. 345, U.P.A. §§ 1, 201, 307 (1997)
Treas. Reg. §§ 1.1378-1, 1.441-1(c), 1.441-1T(b)(2), 1.1643(b)-1, 1.691(a)-1(b), 1.702-1(a)(8)(iii); 1.761-1(a), 1.761-1(b), 301.7701-2; 301.7701-3
Rev. Proc. 2009-50
Ruckman v. Commissioner, T.C. Memo 1998-83
IRS Form 1040 "U.S. Individual Income Tax Return"
Schedules B, C,
IRS Form 1041 "U.S. Income Tax Return for Estates and Trusts"
IRS Form 1065 "U.S. Return of Partnership Income"
Schedule K-1
IRS Form 1099-DIV "Dividends and Distributions"
IRS Form 1099-INT "Interest Income"
IRS Form 1120 "U.S. Corporation Income Tax Return"
IRS Form 1120S "U.S. Income Tax Return for a S Corporation"
IRS Form 2553 "Election by a Small Business Corporation"
Publication 15, (Circular E), Employer's Tax Guide
Publication 15-A, Employer's Supplemental Tax Guide

IRS Publication 542 "Corporations"
IRS Publication 550 "Qualified Dividends"
IRS Publication 583 "Starting a Business and Keeping Records"
Small Business and Self-Employed Tax Center http://www.irs.gov/
businesses/small/index.html
Publication 1779, Independent Contractor or Employee Brochure (PDF)

**A SELF STUDY ASSESSMENT IS AVAILABLE IN THE
ONLINE MATERIALS**

Chapter 10

DEDUCTIONS FOR BUSINESS EXPENSES

Determining what amounts are includible in "gross income" is the starting point in calculating a taxpayer's liability. The next step is to determine what amounts are properly allowed as a deduction from gross income ("above-the-line" deductions) or adjusted gross income (itemized or "below-the-line" deductions).

Broadly speaking, deductions fall into three categories: 1) business/profit-seeking expenses; 2) personal expenses; or 3) mixed business and personal expenses. Personal deductions, which are generally not favored by the Code, are the subject of Chapter 11. This chapter will address the deductibility of expenses incurred for business or profit-seeking activities. Congress provides greater leeway for taxpayers to deduct these expenses because, unlike with personal expenses, these business expenses are incurred as a cost of the taxpayer earning the income. While a taxpayer can choose from a number of different types of entities when conducting a business,[1] this chapter will focus on individuals operating a small business as a sole proprietor.

IRC § 162 allows a deduction for all the "ordinary and necessary" expenses paid or incurred during the taxable year in carrying on any "trade or business." The cases you likely studied in class — *Welch v. Helvering* and *Higgins v. Commissioner* — are the tip of the case law iceberg regarding what is "ordinary and necessary" and what constitutes a "trade or business." In addition, the IRS provides a wealth of administrative guidance to give taxpayers clarity in this area.

An IRC § 162 deduction is an above-the-line deduction, meaning that a taxpayer subtracts the trade or business expenses from gross income to arrive at "adjusted gross income." See IRC § 62(a)(1). Thus, the taxpayer does not have to pay federal income tax on the amounts incurred for business expenses.

One obvious rationale for this favorable treatment is that taxpayers operating as sole proprietors face a myriad of expenses that wage earners do not have to incur personally. For instance, a sole proprietor must buy all of his or her own supplies, carry insurance and sometimes pay employees, while a wage earner typically does not incur these unreimbursed out-of-pocket expenses. Thus it makes sense to allow the sole proprietor to partially recover those costs through an above-the-line deduction.

---

[1] Chapter 9 examines choice of business entity.

Another stark difference in the tax treatment between wage earners and sole proprietors is that the latter are subject to tax on their net self-employment income at a rate totaling 15.3% (12.4 Social Security tax and 2.9% Medicare tax).[2] *See* IRC § 1401. In contrast, wage-earners are subject to FICA taxes totaling only half of that rate — 7.65% (6.2% Social Security tax and a 1.45% Medicare tax) — on their wages. *See* IRC § 3101. The wage-earner's employer is subject to a 7.65% excise tax on the wages paid to each employee, which is intended to match what the employee contributes (note that the employee and employer portions total 15.3%, which is the percentage tax to which a self-employed individual's earnings are subject). *See* IRC § 3111. To alleviate the heavier burden of the 15.3% self-employment tax rate, **IRC § 164(f)** permits an above-the-line deduction for one-half of the self-employment tax. While this does not put the sole proprietor in the same position as the wage earner, it does help offset the higher tax burden by reducing the sole proprietor's gross income.

IRC § 212 allows an individual who is not engaged in a trade or business to deduct certain ordinary and necessary expenses paid or incurred for the production or collection of income. While IRC § 212 provides an opportunity for a taxpayer to recover some costs of earning income, a taxpayer would much rather qualify for an IRC § 162 business expense deduction. Why? One reason is that IRC § 212 deductions are allowed as an itemized deduction,[3] meaning that the taxpayer only benefits from the deduction if his or her itemized deductions exceed the taxpayer's standard deduction. Another reason is that IRC § 212 deductions are among those "miscellaneous itemized deductions" that are subject to the 2% floor of IRC § 67(a). The effect of this is that the taxpayer can only take miscellaneous itemized deductions to the extent that they exceed 2% of the taxpayer's adjusted gross income. Thus, if only allowed an IRC § 212 deduction, a taxpayer recovers less of his incurred expenses than he would if allowed to fully offset them against gross income under IRC § 162.

Certain types of expenses are not solely business expenditures, but are mixed in nature — while there is a business purpose, the taxpayer derives a personal benefit as well. These mixed expenditures receive special scrutiny from the IRS. **IRC § 274** is an example of a Code section that provides special rules for mixed expenditures, placing limitations on the deductibility of business meals and entertainment and imposing strict substantiation requirements. Special rules also apply to limit the deductibility of certain "dual use" property — that is, property used for both business purposes and personal use: **IRC § 280A**

---

[2]   These numbers reflect the IRC § 3101 and § 1401 rates that were in effect in 2010. The Tax Relief, Unemployment Insurance Reauthorization, and Job Creation Act of 2010 created a special one-year "payroll holiday" 2% reduction in the Social Security tax rates. The reduction is intended to stimulate the economy and will occur only for calendar year 2011.

[3]   *See* IRC § 63(d).

restricts the deductibility of a home office, while **IRC § 280F** provides limits on the deductibility of "listed property" (including automobiles, computers, and cell phones) if the property is not predominantly used in the taxpayer's trade or business.

The timing of a deduction for business expenses is another issue that arises. Not all expenses incurred in connection with a trade or business are currently deductible. For example, if a taxpayer purchases a new building for his business, he or she cannot deduct the entire cost of the building in the year of purchase. Nor would a taxpayer likely want to, because there may not be enough current income to enjoy the full benefit of such a deduction. The Code requires many business expenses that are incurred for a long term benefit to be deducted over a longer period of years. These expenses — referred to as capital expenditures — must be recaptured over the useful life of the asset, over an amortization period, or when the property is disposed of.

These rules provide important planning opportunities for a small business owner. A careful understanding of recordkeeping requirements and timing considerations can help a taxpayer maximize profits and minimize problems with the IRS.

Skills Involved: Client counseling, tax planning, using administrative guidance.

General Description of Exercise: Advise a client in the early stages of a new business.

Participants Needed: This is an individual exercise to be completed by one student.

Estimated Time Required: 45 minutes

Level of Difficulty (1-5):

Role in Exercise: A new client seeks your tax-planning advice. She has recently started a licensed daycare in her home and would like your guidance, particularly with respect to allowable deductions.

EXERCISE

Earlier this year, Lucy Jackson began operating a daycare for infants and toddlers in her home. She is operating as a sole proprietor and is a cash-method taxpayer. Her daycare is licensed by the state, and she has one full-time employee named Margaret. After the first several months, Lucy became overwhelmed by the tax implications. She has read a lot of blog postings that suggested she can deduct expenses she had not thought of, like her home and her computer. She is skeptical of these claims because she does not believe everything she reads on the internet. She contacted you to learn more about how to minimize her tax liability.

She provides you with the following facts:

- Lucy pays Margaret $9 an hour, and Margaret works 40 hours per week.

- The daycare is open from 9am until 5pm, Monday to Friday. Lucy closes on the 10 federal holidays during the year and also closes for one week during the summer.

- She currently has 10 children enrolled in her daycare, which is the maximum number she can accommodate under the state regulations for daycare centers. The fee per month is $900 per child. Due to high local demand, she anticipates that enrollment will always be full, and she maintains a waiting list.

- Lucy provides all food or infant formula for the children. Parents are required to provide diapers for the children who need them.

- Way incurs regular expenses for such supplies as paper towels, Kleenex, Clorox, laundry detergent, and Lysol. She estimates these will add up to $1,500 annually.

- The daycare is located in Lucy's primary residence, which is a house that she rents at a cost of $1,500 a month. Her utility costs (electricity, gas, sewage, and trash removal) average $100 per month. She estimates that 1/3 of the space in her house is used in operating the daycare, while the other 2/3 of the house's area is strictly off-limits to the kids and Margaret.

- Lucy is planning to purchase a new laptop computer. She would like your suggestions as to what business use she can make of it and how much personal use is appropriate if she plans to deduct the expense.

In the course of your conversation, Lucy sheepishly tells you that she does not keep a separate checking account for her business — all deposits from the parents go into her personal account, and all expenses (personal and business) are paid from her personal account. She pulls a spiral notebook out of her bag, which contains handwritten notes about payments and expenses. She hands you a recent grocery receipt to show you that she's keeping records for her taxes.

Write Lucy a client letter advising her on the following regarding business expenses: which types of expenses are valid business deductions; whether the deductions are above-the-line or below-the-line; and whether she can deduct any portion of her rent or the cost of a laptop if she buys one in the future. In addition, advise her on best practices for recordkeeping. Consult IRS Publication 587, Business Use of Your Home, for specific guidance on daycare facilities.

REFERENCES — AVAILABLE IN ONLINE MATERIALS

Lucy Jackson's sample receipt
IRC §§ 62(a)(1), 162, 212, 280A, 280F
IRS Publication 334, Tax Guide for Small Businesses
IRS Publication 535, Business Expenses
IRS Publication 583, Starting a Business and Keeping Records
IRS Publication 587, Business Use of Your Home

A SELF STUDY ASSESSMENT IS AVAILABLE IN THE ONLINE MATERIALS

Chapter 11

DEDUCTIONS FOR PERSONAL EXPENSES

Deductions are said to be a matter of "legislative grace."[1] Unlike the broad allowance it has granted for business expenses, Congress has sharply limited deductions for personal expenses. IRC § 262 provides the general rule: "Except as otherwise expressly provided . . . no deduction shall be allowed for personal, living, or family expenses." The Code expressly provides deductions for a number of personal expenses, including: certain types of **personal interest** (IRC § 163(h)); **charitable contributions** (IRC § 170); **medical expenses and health insurance premiums** (IRC § 213); and **qualified tuition expenses** (IRC § 222).

Certain of these deductions for personal expenses are the favored "above-the-line" deductions, while most of these are "below-the-line" deductions that must be itemized. Recall that an above-the-line deduction results in an adjustment to income and is valuable even if the taxpayer takes the standard deduction. On the other hand, "below-the-line" refers to those deductions that are itemized on a Schedule A. Unless the taxpayer chooses to itemize, and those itemized deductions total more than the standard deduction, a below-the-line deduction is of no value to a taxpayer because all taxpayers are allowed a standard deduction regardless of actual expenses.

As with all Code sections, you must take great care when reading the provisions allowing personal deductions. Each provision is replete with requirements, limitations, and exceptions. A tax planner often must take into consideration such additional factors as: the taxpayer's anticipated adjusted gross income; the amount of other anticipated deductions; and whether the taxpayer will itemize.

When advising a taxpayer in matters of tax planning, it is important to remember that a taxpayer will need to be able to substantiate deductions if called upon to do so by the IRS. Some statutory provisions include a strict substantiation requirement. In advising a client — either prospectively or upon audit — you must be familiar with a number of overlapping ethical standards that apply to attorneys practicing before the IRS. The exercises in this chapter will help you to appreciate planning considerations, explore applicable rules of ethics, and contemplate post-filing strategies.

---

[1] *See* New Colonial Ice Co. v. Helvering, 292 U.S. 435, 440 (1934).

Skills Involved: Application of rules of ethics, problem solving, client counseling.

General Description of Exercise: Exercise 1: Consider the ethical implications of the client's revelation; Exercise 2: Devise a strategy for defending the clients at audit.

Participants Needed: This is an individual exercise to be completed by one student.

Estimated Time Required: Exercise 1: 20 minutes; Exercise 2: 20 minutes

Level of Difficulty (1-5):

Role in Exercises: In each exercise, you are called upon to advise a client. Exercise #1 involves an existing client seeking prospective tax planning advice and a review of prior-year returns. Exercise #2 involves counseling a new client in response to an audit of a prior-year return.

EXERCISE #1

During the course of your representation of Thomas and Wendy Taxpayers on other legal matters, the subject of taxes has come up. They wonder whether you know of any deductions that they might be eligible for but are not currently taking. They feel that they pay a lot more income tax than other people, and they would like to be sure that they are claiming every deduction they are entitled to take.

As a starting point, you ask them to provide you with their federal income tax returns for the past three years. In the course of reviewing these returns, you carefully review the taxpayers' Schedule A itemized deductions. Based on what you know about the Taxpayers, you are a bit surprised by what you see on their Schedule A. For instance, their most recent Schedule A includes $12,000 of medical and dental expenses, but you are under the impression that the Taxpayers do not have any health problems. In all, the Taxpayers have claimed Schedule A deductions totaling more than 45% of their income each year. As you talk with the Taxpayers about some of the deductions they have claimed in years past, Thomas makes a variety of comments about how hard he works and how high tax rates are. Thomas then winks and says: "We make sure to get ours back by claiming some things we probably shouldn't. But everyone does that, right?"

What ethical obligations arise upon Thomas's comment? Consider both the Model Rules of Professional Conduct and Treasury Department Circular No. 230.

EXERCISE #2

You are contacted by Jack and Gloria Anderson, a married couple. The Andersons are very upset because they received a letter from the IRS asking for additional information to substantiate certain items that were claimed on their most recent tax return. The Andersons feel that this audit is an attack on their personal integrity, and they wish to do everything they can to prove to the IRS that they did not cheat on their taxes. At issue are the Andersons' deductions for medical expenses and charitable contributions. At your initial meeting, the Andersons explain the deductions to you as follows:

<u>Charitable Contributions</u>: The Andersons claimed $4,350 in charitable contributions in the year at issue; this number was based on figures they wrote down in a notebook each time they made a donation to their church in the tax year. Some of the donations were in cash, but most of them were made by personal check.

<u>Medical Expenses</u>: The Andersons claimed $8,900 in medical expenses. The Andersons have a notebook showing that $2,900 in expenses was incurred for dental visits, co-pays, and prescription drugs. The Andersons have receipts matching some but not all of this $2,900 in expenses. In addition, Jack gives you pay stubs showing that his employer had withheld $500 per month for health insurance premiums as part of an employer-sponsored plan that covered both of the Andersons. These premiums account for the additional $6,000 of medical expenses claimed.

Upon examining Jack's Form W-2, you conclude that the $500 monthly premiums are a pre-tax reduction in salary. These amounts are not included in box 1 of Jack's Form W-2 (i.e., the premiums were paid with money that is not included in Jack's gross income).

Review the applicable statutory provisions and devise a strategy for the Andersons to reply to the IRS correspondence. Provide them with any additional tax planning advice for future years.

REFERENCES — AVAILABLE IN ONLINE MATERIALS

IRC §§ 62, 63, 170, 213, 262
Sample Letter 566 and Form 886-A
IRS Publication 502, Medical and Dental Expenses
ABA Model Rules of Professional Conduct Rule 1.6 Confidentiality
of Information
Treasury Department Circular 230 §§ 10.21, 10.22, 10.51(a)(7)

A SELF STUDY ASSESSMENT IS AVAILABLE IN THE ONLINE MATERIALS

Chapter 12

DEFERRAL AND NON-RECOGNITION PROVISIONS

This chapter examines some of the various deferral and non-recognition provisions in the Code. It is strategically placed toward the end of the book because these concepts require a general understanding of the underlying substantive rules. The exercises in this chapter are by no means exhaustive of the different deferral and non-recognition provisions in the Code, however, they are intended to give you a general framework to assist with your understanding of these technical rules, how they arise in certain circumstances, and how they are reported to the Internal Revenue Service.

In general, there are two types of non-recognition provisions: (1) non-recognition of gain or loss on the transfer of property from one taxpayer to another and (2) the acquisition of one property in exchange for another. Many of these provisions intersect with other sections in the Code, making the application of these rules technical and often complex.

Transfers of Property from One Taxpayer to Another

Transfers between Spouses. As set forth in more detail in Chapter 8, during marriage, a husband and wife are treated as a single economic unit. Accordingly, the general rule under IRC § 1041 is that no gain or loss shall be recognized on transfers between spouses, or a former spouse when incident to divorce. When this rule applies, the transfer is treated as a gift and the transferee spouse always takes a carryover basis.[1] This is a "non-recognition" rule that is non-elective. Even when one spouse sells property to another, no gain or loss on the sale is recognized. The tax is deferred until the subsequent sale of the property (see exercises in Chapter 8).

Gifts. As discussed in Chapter 5, when property is acquired by gift, the donee of the gift acquires the transferor's adjusted basis in the property, which is commonly referred to as carryover basis.[2] This is relevant for income tax purposes because, when the donee of the gift later sells or transfers the asset, the gain or loss on the asset or subsequent basis in the new donee's hands will depend (in most cases) on the original transferor's adjusted basis in the asset. The tax is deferred until the subsequent sale of the property (see exercises in Chapter 5).

---

[1] IRC § 1041(b)(1). The Treasury Regulations require that the transferor spouse provide basis and holding period information to the transferee spouse at the time of the transfer to ensure proper recordkeeping. Treas. Reg. §1.1041-1T(e), Q & A-14.
[2] IRC § 1015.

Transfers between Related Parties. Related party transactions arise in many different contexts and often delay or postpone the recognition of a loss on the sale of property to a related taxpayer. In general, IRC § 267(a)(1) provides that no deduction will be allowed with respect to a loss from the sale or exchange of property, directly or indirectly, between persons that are specified in any part of § 267(b). These related party rules are triggered upon transfers between two or more family members, controlled entities or between an entity and equity holder.[3] The theory behind the related party rules is to prevent the shifting of losses or the creation of a loss on an asset that has not sufficiently left the taxpayer's control. If there would have been a recognizable loss on the sale, but for the related party rules, IRC § 267(d) provides that to the extent that the transferee later sells the property, there will be no recognition of gain to the extent of the previous disallowance of loss.[4] Thus the loss on the property is postponed until the subsequent sale of the property.

Transfers of Property in an Exchange

Like Kind Exchanges. IRC § 1031(a) provides that no gain or loss shall be recognized on a "like kind" exchange of qualifying property held for productive use in a trade or business or for investment if such property is exchanged solely for property of like kind which is to be held either for productive use in a trade or business or for investment. "Like kind" refers to the nature or character of the property and not to its grade or quality.[5] To be considered like kind, IRC § 1031(a)(3) provides certain time limits within which the property has to be identified and exchanged. As with the other non-recognition provisions discussed in this chapter, the tax is not eliminated, but rather deferred until the subsequent sale of the qualifying property.

The theory behind the non-recognition provisions of IRC § 1031 is that with an exchange of qualifying property, unlike a sale, the taxpayer has not yet realized the return on the investment. It would be unfair to force the taxpayer to recognize the tax until the economic gain on the asset has been realized. There are circumstances, however, when gain is recognized under a 1031 exchange. If the exchange includes like kind property along with cash, liabilities, and property that is not like kind, there may be taxable gain in the year of exchange.[6]

If the transaction qualifies as a like kind exchange under IRC § 1031, the taxpayer's original basis in the property is preserved and the basis of property acquired in a § 1031 exchange is the same as the basis of the property transferred, decreased by the amount of any money received and increased by the amount of any gain recognized. For purposes of IRC § 1031(d), where, as part of the consideration to the taxpayer,

---

[3]   IRC § 267(b), (c).
[4]   Treas. Reg. § 1.267(d)-1(a)(1).
[5]   Treas. Reg. § 1.1031(a)-1(b).
[6]   IRC § 1031(b).

another party to the exchange assumes a liability of the taxpayer, such assumption shall be considered as money received by the taxpayer on the exchange. Using the taxpayer's basis in the transferred property as the starting point of the basis determination preserves any gain or loss in the property, which will be recognized upon the subsequent sale or exchange (other than a like kind exchange) of the property.

Like kind exchanges between related parties are permissible under IRC § 1031, however, they are subject to the holding rules in IRC § 1031(f). To avoid the shifting of basis between related taxpayers, IRC § 1031(f) requires a two-year holding period after an exchange between related parties. The rules provide that if either the taxpayer or the related party disposes of the exchanged property within two years, then the taxpayer's exchange with the related party becomes taxable in the subsequent year of sale. There are certain exceptions to this rule, including upon the death of one of the parties to the exchange.[7]

Installment Sales. When a taxpayer sells property, the taxpayer typically recognizes gain or loss at the time of the sale.[8] If property is sold at a gain and the proceeds are received at a later time, however, IRC § 453 provides that the gain on the sale and the associated tax liability are spread over the period during which the payments are received. An installment sale is defined under IRC § 453(b)(1) as a disposition of property where at least one payment is to be received after the close of the taxable year in which the disposition occurs. The installment sale rules under IRC § 453(c) require that the gain on the sale of the asset be pro-rated over the total payments to be received and the amount includable in income is based on the gross profit percentage. The gross profit percentage ratio is calculated as follows:

$$\frac{\text{Gross Profit}}{\text{Contract Price}}$$

Gross profit is defined as the selling price less the adjusted basis.[9] The contract price is defined as the selling price less mortgages that do not exceed basis.[10] In installment sales, mortgages and other liabilities assumed are not deemed to be a payment to the seller to the extent they do not exceed the basis in the property.[11] To the extent that a mortgage or other assumed liabilities exceed basis, the excess will be included in the contract price and will increase the percentage of the payments that must be included in income as they are repaid. A taxpayer can elect out of the installment sale method under § 453(d) and report the income under the usual method of accounting. Finally, under IRC § 453(e), the amount realized on the disposition of property acquired in an installment

---

[7] IRC § 1031(f)(2)(a).
[8] IRC § 1001(c).
[9] Treas. Reg. § 15A.453-1(b)(2)(iii).
[10] *Id.*
[11] *Id.*

sale from a related party within two years of the related party sale will be treated as a payment to the original related party seller.

Skills Involved: Fact analysis, problem solving, application of statutes, understanding tax forms.

General Description of Exercises: Installment Sale, Reporting and Related Parties; Like Kind Exchange and Sale of a Personal Residence.

Participants Needed: This is an individual exercise to be completed by one student.

Estimated Time Required: Exercise 1: Task 1: 30 minutes, Task 2: 20 minutes; Exercise 2: 30 minutes

Level of Difficulty (1-5):

Role in Exercise: Tax lawyer

EXERCISE # 1

Mary lost her job half-way through the year in 2009 and has had trouble finding work, so she has decided to sell a painting that she bought in 1995 for $10,000 to generate some income. On November 12, 2009, she sold the painting to her brother Jack for $20,000, payable in monthly installments over the next three years with an interest rate of 7%. Mary would like to discuss the income tax consequences of the sale. You have run the numbers for her and have determined that the repayment schedule will consist of monthly payments in the amount of $617.54, which are comprised of principal and income payments as follows:

Tax Year	Payment	Interest	Principal
2009	$617.54	$116.67	$500.87
2010	$7,410.48	$1,167.16	$6,243.32
2011	$7,410.48	$715.81	$6,694.67
2012	$6,793.00	$231.86	$6,561.14
Total	**$22,231.50**	**$2,231.50**	**$20,000**

Task # 1: Mary is coming to your office next week to discuss the tax consequences of the sale to her brother. How will you advise Mary on how to report the income from the sale of the painting? What forms does she need to use to report the income and how much of the income will be reported on her return in 2009 and in 2010? In preparation for your meeting, prepare Form 6252 Installment Sale Income (online). This form will guide you in your discussion with Mary.

Task #2: About a year later, Jack sold the paining to an unrelated buyer, and Mary remembers that you told her about the related party rules, but she cannot for the life of her remember what you said. What are the tax consequences to Mary, if any, when Jack sells the painting at the end of 2010?

EXERCISE #2

Andrew Smith has come to you for advice on the tax consequences of an exchange of property. Andrew bought a house for $210,000 that he used as his principal residence from 2004 to 2008. From 2008 until 2010, Andrew rented the house to tenants and claimed depreciation deductions of $20,000. In 2010, he exchanged the house for $10,000 of cash and a townhouse with a fair market value of $460,000 that Andrew intends to rent to tenants. He wants to know what the tax consequences are. Other than his rental property and wages, he does not have a ton of extra cash to pay tax on gain inherent in this exchange so he is concerned about the tax consequences.

Assume that the exchange would qualify for a 1031 exchange because the property is used by the transferor in a trade or business or for the production of income and the property to be received will be used in a trade or business or for the production of income. In addition, assume that the properties to be exchanged are of like kind and eligible for exchange without recognition of gain or loss under § 1031. Finally, you should consider the impact of IRC § 121 on this transaction. Does IRC § 121 impact the amount that is deferred? Does it impact Andrew's basis in the townhouse? Do the rules in IRC § 121(d)(5)(B) provide any guidance?

REFERENCES — AVAILABLE IN ONLINE MATERIALS

Jones 1040, Schedule B
IRC §§ 121, 267, 453, 1001(a), § 1015, 1031, 1041,
Treas. Reg. §§ 1.267(d)-1(a)(1), 1.1002-1, 1.1031(a)-1(b), 1.1031(a)-2,
1.1041-1T(e), Q & A-14, 15A.453-1(b)(2)(iii)
Rev. Proc. 2005-14
IRS Form 1040 "U.S. Individual Income Tax Return"
IRS Form 4797 "Sales of Business Property"
IRS Form 6252 "Installment Sale Income"
IRS Form 8824 "Like Kind Exchanges"

IRS Publication 17 "Your Federal Income Tax"
IRS Publication 523 "Selling your Home — Reporting the Sale"
IRS Publication 537 "Installment Sales"
IRS Publication 544 "Sales and Other Disposition of Assets"

**A SELF STUDY ASSESSMENT IS AVAILABLE IN THE
ONLINE MATERIALS**

Chapter 13
TAX PROCEDURE AND ADMINISTRATION

In subtle but important ways, the rules of tax procedure affect all of the cases you will read this semester. Regardless of whether an attorney is a tax planner advising on prospective transactions or a litigator representing clients in post-filing controversies, it is important to know how to navigate the various statutory provisions concerning filing deadlines and statutes of limitations.

The Code's administrative provisions are mostly within Subtitle F of the Code, titled "Procedure and Administration" (see IRC §§ 6001-7874). Entire treatises are devoted to the particulars of tax procedure; however, this chapter and its exercises are intended only to introduce you to the most fundamental and widely relevant rules. Each rule has a number of applicable exceptions, only a sampling of which are mentioned here, and administrative guidance and/or case law also supplement each of these basic rules.

Basic Filing Requirements

Most taxpayers do not look to the Code to determine whether, where, and when they must file a return. It is not necessary to do so, as the IRS provides plenty of administrative guidance in its publications and form instructions. For example, the IRS website routinely offers a feature called "Do You Need to File a Federal Income Tax Return?"

But it is of course the Code that provides the fundamental statutory framework for who must file a return and when. IRC § 6012 describes who is required to file a return, and also provides an exception for individuals with gross income below a set amount (generally the sum of the taxpayer's exemption amount plus the applicable standard deduction). It is IRC § 6072 that mandates the well-known April 15th filing deadline for a taxpayer to submit a tax return for the prior calendar year. IRC § 6081 grants the Treasury Secretary the authority to grant filing extensions, while IRC § 6091 provides the Secretary the authority to prescribe the place for the filing of returns.

As this chapter will show, the date of filing can have great significance — but when is a return considered "filed"? Is it filed when mailed by the taxpayer or when received by the IRS? The date of "filing" depends upon whether the return was mailed before or after the due date. A return that is mailed either before or on the due date for the return will be considered "filed" as of the due date, even if it is received by the IRS after the due date. *See* IRC §§ 6501(b)(1), 6513(a), 7502.

The special rule of IRC § 7503 applies when a due date falls on a Saturday, Sunday, or legal holiday. In that case, the filing is still considered timely as long as it is mailed on the next succeeding business day. For example, if April 15 falls on a Saturday, a return due by April 15th is considered timely filed if it is mailed on Monday, April 17th. On the other hand, a return that is mailed on Tuesday, April 18th, is deemed "filed" only upon receipt by the IRS, not on the date mailed.

Assessment

After a taxpayer files an income tax return, the IRS assesses the tax as determined and reported by the taxpayer.[1] This is sometimes referred to as "self-assessment," because the IRS is merely formalizing what the taxpayer reported to the IRS. The date that the return is filed is significant, as it triggers the start of the statute of limitations for the IRS to assess a tax liability. The general statute of limitations for assessment is three years from the date the return was filed.[2] This provides closure for the taxpayer who files tax returns and in most cases, the IRS cannot look back at a return to make an additional assessment once three years has passed since the due date or later date of filing.

This general three-year rule has significant exceptions. In the following cases, the IRS may assess tax at any time (in other words, no statute of limitations exists on assessment under these circumstances): 1) the filing of "a false or fraudulent return with the intent to evade tax"; 2) a "willful attempt in any manner to defeat or evade tax"; or 3) the failure to file a tax return.[3]

Another exception to the three-year rule provides an alternative six-year statute of limitations for assessment in the case of a taxpayer who makes a "substantial omission" of items of gross income. The general rule is that when a taxpayer omits gross income that exceeds 25% of the gross income reported on the return, the IRS has six years to assess the tax.[4]

When advising a taxpayer, it is important to look for and appreciate any intervening events that might have suspended the statute of limitations on assessment. For example, IRC § 6503(a) provides that the applicable statute of limitations for assessment is suspended if the IRS files a Notice of Deficiency. This is because during this time, the IRS is prohibited from making an assessment. Similarly, the statute for assessment is suspended if a taxpayer files for bankruptcy.[5] In a different vein, the taxpayer might have voluntarily consented to extend the statute of limitations on assessment by signing Form 872.[6] A practitioner can

---

[1] *See* IRC § 6201(a)(1).
[2] *See* IRC § 6501(a).
[3] *See* IRC § 6501(c).
[4] *See* IRC § 6501(e)(1)(A).
[5] *See* IRC § 6503(h).
[6] *See* IRC § 6501(c)(4).

usually determine the occurrence of these events by reading the taxpayer's IRS account transcript.

Once the tax has been properly (and timely) assessed, the IRS can begin collection efforts, which are governed by a separate statute of limitations.

Collection

The administrative mechanisms available to the IRS for the collection of taxes — the procedural details of which are beyond the scope of this chapter — include refund offsets, liens, and levies. However the IRS is temporally constrained in its collection efforts by IRC § 6502, which generally provides that the IRS must collect the tax through administrative means or bring a judicial proceeding for such collection within 10 years from the date of the assessment.[7] This 10-year period ends on what is known as the "collection statute expiration date." If the IRS cannot collect the tax or does not institute a judicial proceeding before the collection statute expiration date, it must release any liens and remove the balance due from the taxpayer's account.

A number of statutorily specified events will suspend the collection statute expiration date. Typically these events also prevent the IRS from pursuing collection or that hamper its efforts. Some of the same rules mentioned with respect to suspending the statute of limitations for assessment also apply to the statute for collection. For example, the collection statute is suspended when a taxpayer files for bankruptcy or files a petition in Tax Court. Other provisions apply to suspend the statute on collection, but do not suspend the statute of limitations for assessment; an example of this is IRC § 6503(c), which suspends the statute of limitations for collections when the taxpayer is outside the United States for a period of at least six months. In some cases, a taxpayer agrees to suspend the collections statute upon invoking an administrative procedure, such as filing an Offer in Compromise[8] or requesting a Collection Due Process Hearing.

Claim for a Refund

As you have learned, the IRS does not have an unlimited amount of time to assess tax after a return is filed, nor does it have an unlimited amount of time to collect tax after it is assessed. These statutory limitations protect taxpayers and provide them with certainty and, eventually, closure, as to their tax liabilities. But what about the IRS?

---

[7] Note that the statute of limitations for collections is started by the act of the IRS assessing the tax, not by the act of the taxpayer filing. Assessment is an administrative act performed by the Service. Accordingly, even if the IRS accepts the taxpayer's "self-assessment" as correct, the taxpayer cannot be certain of the actual date of assessment without viewing the IRS account transcript.

[8] See Form 656, Offer in Compromise, § V(e), which has the taxpayer acknowledge the suspension of the statutory period for collection as a term of submitting the Offer. See also IRC § 6331(k) and Treas. Reg. 301.7122-1(i), which provide that the statute for collection is suspended while levy is prohibited.

Is it allowed administrative closure, or is a taxpayer allowed to claim a refund at any time?

In this regard, IRC § 6511 could be viewed as a parallel rule to the limitation on assessment in IRC § 6501 because it provides a limitation on the period a taxpayer has to file a claim for a credit or refund of an overpayment. The general rule, which is somewhat confusing at first blush, states that a "[c]laim for credit or refund of an overpayment . . . shall be filed by the taxpayer within three years from the time the return was filed or two years from the time the tax was paid, whichever of such periods expires the later."

A straightforward application of the rule is as follows: a taxpayer filed a timely return and paid the balance due with the return, then subsequently filed an amended return as a refund claim. In this case, the taxpayer will only receive a refund if the amended return is filed within three years of the time that the original return was filed.[9] The amount of any refund may be limited by IRC § 6511(b), which states that the amount of the refund shall not exceed the portion of the tax paid within the three-year period. For this purpose, payments including withholding and estimated tax payments that were made before the filing deadline are considered to be "paid" on the filing deadline.[10] Hence, if a taxpayer filed his 2006 return by April 15, 2007, he has until April 19, 2010 to file a timely claim for a refund.

Take a close look at IRC § 6511 to see how it applies slightly differently to a delinquent filer: a taxpayer who has not filed a timely return, but is due a refund, must file within three years of the return's (disregarded) original due date in order to receive the refund. In this case, the three years is significant not because of the IRC § 6511(a) time limit for filing a claim (which will not bar the claim), but because of the IRC § 6511(b)(2)(A) limit on amount of credit or refund.[11] In other words, if a taxpayer did not file a return for 2006 until April 20, 2010, the IRC § 6511(a) period of limitation begins running when the return is filed on April 20, 2010. Therefore, the *claim* for the refund is timely. However, under IRC § 6511(b)(2)(A), the *amount* of the refund is limited to the amount of tax paid during the period April 20, 2007 to April 20, 2010. In this case, because no tax for 2006 was paid during that period, there is no amount eligible for a refund.

The two-year rule might arise where more than three years have passed since the due date of the return, but payments (including a levy) have been made on an assessed deficiency. If the taxpayer files a claim for a refund, IRC § 6511(b)(2)(B) provides that the amount of the refund will be limited to the portion of the tax paid during the two years immediately preceding the filing of the refund claim.

---

[9] Similar to the IRC § 6501(b)(1) rule for determining the filing date for assessment purposes, IRC § 6513(a) provides that an early return is considered to be filed on the due date.

[10] *See* IRC § 6513(b)(1).

[11] *See* Rev. Rul. 76–511.

As with the other types of statutes of limitations, certain exceptions apply that could potentially suspend the IRC § 6511 period of limitation.

Penalties

To promote voluntary compliance, Congress has granted the IRS the authority to impose various types of civil penalties. Worth a brief mention in this chapter is IRC § 6551, which authorizes the IRS to impose penalties for failure to file a tax return and failure to pay tax.

IRC § 6651(a)(1) authorizes a substantial penalty for failure to file a timely return: 5% of the amount of tax required to be shown on the return if the failure is for not more than one month, with an additional 5% for each additional month or fraction thereof, not exceeding 25% in the aggregate. Because the penalty is determined as a percentage of the tax due, there will be no penalty charged if a refund or a no balance-due return is filed late.

IRC § 6651(a)(2) authorizes a separate penalty for failure to pay the tax due on or before the due date of the return. The penalty is calculated as .5% of the tax if failure is not for more than one month, with an additional .5% for each additional month or fraction thereof, not exceeding 25% in the aggregate.[12]

An obvious, and significant, disparity exists between those penalties — the failure to file penalty is ten times the rate (per month) of the failure to pay penalty. Thus it is almost certainly in a taxpayer's best interest to file a balance-due return on a timely basis regardless of whether he pays the amount due.

Skills Involved: Statutory analysis, applying deadlines

General Description of Exercise: A series of quiz questions meant to familiarize you with basic tax procedure provisions.

Participants Needed: This is an individual exercise to be completed by one student.

Estimated Time Required: 20 minutes

---

[12] IRC § 6651(c) provides that the failure-to-file penalty may be reduced by the amount of the failure-to-pay penalty when both apply in the same month; the practical effect of this is that the combined penalties will not exceed 5% in a given month.

Level of Difficulty (1-5):

Role in Exercise: Consider each question, research the answer, and then check your answers online.

EXERCISE

1) Client filed her 2008 income tax return timely by mailing it on March 18, 2009. She received a refund shortly thereafter. On her return, she claimed the earned income tax credit, for which she met all of the requirements. She has kept records of the appropriate documentation just in case the IRS questions her return.

   What is the minimum amount of time for which Client should retain these records?

   a) Until March 18, 2012
   b) Until April 15, 2012
   c) Until April 15, 2015
   d) Until March 18, 2019

2) On May 1, 2009, Client mailed his 2008 tax return, which showed a balance due of $5,400. Client did not make any payment, as he could not afford the balance due.

   How much time does the IRS have to collect the balance due — in other words, when is the collection statute expiration date?

3) Same facts as question 2, but Client submitted an Offer in Compromise in the summer of 2010. His offer was pending as of July 1, 2010. It was rejected by the IRS on September 30, 2010.

   When is the collection statute expiration date?

4) Clients, a married couple with three children, have not filed tax returns for the last decade. To help bring them into filing compliance, you prepare federal income tax returns for the current and past several years, including 2004, 2005, 2006, 2007, 2008, and 2009. Clients come in to sign the returns on April 14, 2010, and you mail the returns to the IRS that same day. Clients were greatly surprised to learn that they would have been due a refund on all of those returns. Now they are eager to know how much money they will get back.

For which tax years are taxpayers eligible to receive their refund?

a) The current year only: 2009

b) All years: 2004–2009

c) The most recent four years: 2006–2009

d) The most recent three years: 2007–2009

REFERENCES — AVAILABLE IN ONLINE MATERIALS

Sample Account Transcript showing expiration of CSED
Sample Account Transcript showing suspension of CSED

IRC §§ 6201, 6501, 6503, 6511, 6513, 6651, 7502, 7503
Treas. Reg. § 301.7502-1(f)

U.S. Tax Court website: http://www.ustaxcourt.gov/
Form 656, Offer in Compromise
Form 1040X, Amended U.S. Individual Income Tax Return

A SELF STUDY ASSESSMENT IS AVAILABLE IN THE ONLINE MATERIALS

Chapter 14
INTERNATIONAL TAX

You have spent the semester learning about the federal income tax system. You have explored the definition of "income," studied statutory exclusions from gross income, and examined provisions allowing various deductions. You now know a great deal of detail about how the United States taxes the income of individuals. But which individuals are subject to U.S. tax: all individuals present in the United States, regardless of citizenship? What about U.S. citizens living abroad?

This chapter will introduce you to the foundational principles of what is often called "international tax." This term, however, is somewhat of a misnomer because there is no international taxing body. In the United States, "international tax" is often used as shorthand for the study of the Code provisions involving: 1) the taxation of U.S. persons who receive income from sources outside the United States (often referred to as "outbound transactions"); and 2) the taxation of foreign persons who receive income from sources inside the United States (often referred to as "inbound transactions").

IRC § 1 imposes an income tax on an "individual." Treasury Regulation § 1.1-1 provides that section 1 applies to "every individual who is a citizen or resident of the United States and, to the extent provided by section 871(b) or 877(b), on the income of a nonresident alien individual." IRC § 2(d) explicitly limits the scope of § 1, providing that: "[i]n the case of a nonresident alien individual, the taxes imposed by section 1 . . . shall apply only as provided by section 871 or 877." Thus it is crucial to understand the difference between a "U.S. citizen or resident" and a "nonresident alien individual."

Who is a "U.S. Resident"?

IRC § 7701(a)(30)(A) defines "U.S. person" as including "a citizen or resident of the United States." The term "citizen" has the same meaning in tax law as it does for purposes of immigration law (see Treas. Reg. § 1.1-1(c), which provides a cross-reference to the Immigration and Nationality Act). In contrast, the Code supplies its own definition of "resident" solely for tax purposes. IRC § 7701(b)(1)(A) provides a bright-line definition of "resident alien": if an individual meets the requirements of any of three alternative clauses (i)–(iii), that person shall be treated as a resident alien for tax purposes.

Test 1: The first clause is often referred to as the "green card test": an individual who is a lawful permanent resident of the United States (in accordance with immigration law) is a U.S. resident for tax purposes.[1] This test is easy to administer and provides great certainty for taxpayers. The practical effect is that lawful permanent residents are treated the same as U.S. citizens for tax purposes — both are subject to tax on their worldwide income from all sources regardless of where the taxpayer actually lives. If the lawful permanent resident status is later rescinded or administratively or judicially determined to have been abandoned, the person will no longer be a U.S. resident for tax purposes.[2]

Test 2: The second clause, IRC § 7701(b)(1)(A)(ii), is commonly referred to as the "substantial presence test." The threshold question is whether the individual was present in the United States on at least 31 days during the calendar year.[3] If so, the substantial presence test employs a formula that considers the actual number of days the individual is present in the United States during the current year, and the number of days he or she is present in the United States in the two preceding calendar years subject to a multiplier. If the sum of the number of days equals or exceeds 183 days, the individual is a resident for the calendar year.

Using the multiplier for the preceding years, each day in the second preceding year counts as $1/6$ of a day and each day in the preceding year counts as $1/3$ of a day. Thus, although the substantial presence test considers a three-year span of time, it also weighs presence in older years less than presence in the current year. The following example illustrates the application of the substantial presence test: In 2009, Jennifer spent a total of 98 days in the United States. In 2008, she spent a total of 135 days in the United States. In 2007, she spent a total of 156 days in the United States. Jennifer does not meet the substantial presence test in 2009 because, applying the 7701(b)(3)(A)(ii) formula, she was in the United States for 169 days in the past three calendar years. The calculation is as follows: $98 + (135 * 1/3) + (156 * 1/6)$. Because Jennifer fails to meet the substantial presence test, she is not a resident alien. On the other hand, if Jennifer had spent 112 days in the United States in 2009, she would be a U.S. resident for tax purposes $(112 + (135 * 1/3) + (156 * 1/6) = 183$ days).

Test 3: The third clause, IRC § 7701(b)(1)(A)(iii), is an election rather than a test. An individual who does not otherwise qualify as a "U.S. resident" but who meets specific criteria can elect to be treated as a U.S. resident for tax purposes.

Though it is intended as a bright-line test to provide certainty to nonresident alien individuals, IRC § 7701(b) is riddled with exceptions and special rules. For instance, IRC § 7701(b)(3)(D)(i) provides that "exempt individuals" (as defined in IRC § 7701(b)(5)) shall not be

---

[1]   IRC § 7701(b)(1)(A)(i).
[2]   Treas. Reg. § 301.7701(b)-1(b).
[3]   IRC § 7701(b)(3)(A)(i).

treated as being present in the United States on any day for which they are exempt. Consequently, exempt individuals (a category that includes certain teachers, students, and diplomats, among others) can be in the United States for more than half a year (183 days) and still not meet the substantial presence test.

Another example of an exception to the substantial presence test is the special rule applicable to individuals who are unable to leave the United States because of a medical condition that arose during their stay.[4] Yet another exception is available to certain qualifying individuals who have a "closer connection" to a foreign country.[5] As these examples illustrate, when making the determination that an individual is a U.S. resident, it is not enough to simply know how many days that person has spent in the United States.

As you might imagine, the application of IRC § 7701(b) can have results that are surprising to those who have studied immigration law. For example, an individual with no immigration status (i.e., an undocumented worker) can be a "U.S. resident" for tax purposes, while an individual lawfully in the United States on a student visa (in compliance with the terms of subparagraph (F) of § 101(15) of the Immigration and Nationality Act) is an "exempt individual," and thus a "nonresident alien" for tax purposes. This is true even if the student has lived exclusively in the United States for five years.[6]

Who is a "Nonresident Alien"?

IRC § 7701(b)(1)(B) provides that an individual is a nonresident alien if he or she is neither a U.S. citizen nor a U.S resident within the meaning of IRC § 7701(b)(1)(A). Thus, this is effectively a residual rule: if a noncitizen individual is not within the definition of "resident alien," he or she is by default a nonresident alien.

Outbound Transactions — (a.k.a. The Taxation of a U.S. Person's Income From Foreign Sources)

U.S. citizens and resident aliens are subject to tax by the United States on their worldwide income regardless of source.[7] Thus, a U.S. person generally continues to be subject to tax under IRC § 1 when he or she moves to a different country. In *Cook v.Tait,*[8] the Supreme Court held that citizenship-based taxation did not violate the Constitution.

At the same time, many countries tax income arising from sources within their country. Because of the United States' broad jurisdiction to

---

4   *See* IRC § 7701(b)(3)(D)(ii); Treas. Reg. § 301.7701(b)-3(c).
5   *See* IRC § 7701(b)(3)(B); Treas. Reg. § 301.7701(b)-2.
6   *See* IRC § 7701(b)(5)(D), (E)(ii).
7   Treas. Reg. § 1.1-1(b).
8   265 U.S. 47 (1924).

tax citizens and resident aliens living abroad, many of these individuals suffer from "double taxation" — a tax liability in two or more countries arising from the same income. The Code provides statutory mechanisms to relieve or eliminate the effects of this "double taxation." The primary means of relief are the foreign tax credit (IRC § 901) and the foreign earned income exclusion (IRC § 911). The mechanics of these provisions are beyond the scope of this introduction, but it is important to know that such relief is available.

Inbound Transactions — (a.k.a. The Taxation Of a Foreign Person's Income From U.S. Sources)

Nonresident aliens are subject to a much more limited form of taxation compared to that applied to resident aliens and citizens. Very generally, IRC § 871 provides that the United States can tax two types of income derived by nonresident aliens: 1) income effectively connected with a U.S. trade or business; and 2) certain types of U.S.-source nonbusiness income. This chapter is not meant as a detailed explanation of the types of income that fall under IRC § 871 or the source rules contained in the Code. For our purposes, it is sufficient to note that the Code requires a jurisdictional nexus as a prerequisite to the taxation by the United States of income derived by nonresident aliens. The primary (but not exclusive) nexus is the source of the income. The United States generally does not have the jurisdiction to tax foreign-source income derived by nonresident aliens.

Effect of Income Tax Treaties

Although the Code sets forth the rules for the taxation of income derived by nonresident aliens, the analysis does not necessarily end there. The United States has entered into bilateral income tax treaties with over 50 nations, and the Code provisions are applied to a taxpayer "with due regard to any treaty obligation." IRC § 894(a). Among other things, income tax treaties provide rules that a taxpayer can elect to apply as an alternative to those set forth in the Code. While each actual treaty is individually negotiated and thus differs in its terms, the starting point for U.S. negotiations is set out in the U.S. Model Income Tax Treaty.

A primary function of income tax treaties is to avoid double taxation; treaties do so by assigning jurisdiction to tax to either the source country (i.e., the country in which the item of income arises) or the residence country (i.e., the country in which the taxpayer is a resident). In some cases, a treaty will allow both the country of source and the country of residence to tax an item of income, with the country of source withholding at a rate set forth in the treaty that is generally less than its rate under its internal law. Although each treaty varies in its specific terms, the general trend in treaties negotiated by developed countries such as the United States is to allocate the jurisdiction to tax to the country of residence. Accordingly, these treaties often reduce or eliminate source-based taxation.

The result of this trend is that income tax treaties generally have a significant impact on inbound transactions and are of very limited use for outbound transactions. It is useful to note that a U.S. person generally cannot use a U.S. income tax treaty to reduce U.S. taxation.[9] On the other hand, a nonresident alien who can elect treaty benefits may be entitled to a reduced rate of tax on certain U.S. source income, and in some cases, certain income may be exempt from withholding tax altogether.

Treaties are organized by articles, and various types of income are addressed individually in these articles. The U.S. Model Treaty, for example, includes different provisions for the following types of "non-business" income: dividends (Article 10); interest (Article 11); and royalties (Article 12). Article 14 governs the treatment of income from employment. Articles 5 ("Permanent Establishment") and 7 ("Business Profits") address the treatment of business income.

Treaty benefits apply at the election of the taxpayer. When analyzing a nonresident alien's potential U.S. tax liability, it makes sense to first determine the tax liability under the Code, and then analyze whether an applicable treaty might reduce or eliminate that liability. IRC § 6114 and the regulations thereunder (Treas. Reg. § 301.6114-1) require a taxpayer to disclose certain treaty-based positions on his or her tax return.

Skills Involved: Fact analysis, problem-solving, application of statutes, income tax treaty interpretation.

General Description of Exercise: Determine whether each taxpayer is a U.S. resident or a nonresident alien; advise each taxpayer as to how residency may impact U.S. taxation; consider the potential application of an income tax treaty.

Participants Needed: This is an individual exercise to be completed by one student.

Estimated Time Required: Task 1: 25 minutes; Task 2: 15 minutes; Task 3: 15 minutes

---

[9] Treaties generally include a "saving clause" preserving the right of a party to the treaty to tax its residents — and in the case of the United States, its citizens — as though the treaty had not entered into force. This limits the extent to which a resident or citizen can claim treaty benefits to saving clause exceptions set forth in the treaty. See, for example, Article 1, paragraph 4 of the U.S. Model Income Tax Treaty, which provides: "Except to the extent provided in paragraph 5, this Convention shall not affect the taxation by a Contracting State of its residents (as determined under Article 4 (Resident)) and its citizens."

Level of Difficulty (1-5):

Role in Exercise: Anne, a foreign national, has contacted you to ask whether she might have any U.S. tax consequences due to the time she spent in the United States during 2009. She would also like tax-planning advice for the year 2010 and beyond.

EXERCISE

Anne is a citizen of Denmark. She is not a U.S. citizen, nor is she a U.S. permanent resident, but in recent years she has spent a lot of time in the United States. For all of the years in question, Anne has been an employee at a Copenhagen-based corporation, earning an annual salary of approximately $65,000. The corporation does not have a permanent establishment in the United States. Anne owns an apartment in Copenhagen; she also keeps her car and personal belongings in Copenhagen. She is a member of a tennis club in Copenhagen, and she is subject to Denmark's income tax as a resident of Denmark. She votes in Denmark.

Anne's sister, her only living family member, lives in Florida. Typically, Anne travels to Florida each August to spend two weeks with her sister. In recent years, however, Anne's sister has been quite ill; as a result, Anne has been spending extended periods of time in Florida. Anne spent a total of 114 days in Florida in 2009. In 2008, she spent a total of 126 days in Florida. In 2007, she spent a total of 150 days in Florida. Anne tells you that she might need to spend a longer period in Florida in 2010.

In addition to her $65,000 salary, Anne received the following types of income in the tax year 2009: $1,500 of U.S.-source interest income; $2,000 of U.S.-source dividend income; and $7,000 of foreign-source dividend income.

TASK #1

Determine whether Anne is a "U.S. resident" for tax purposes in 2009. Regardless of whether she is a U.S. resident in 2009, consider whether Anne might be subject to taxation in the United States on any of her income.

Once you determine the answer under the Code, consider whether Anne might wish to elect benefits under an income tax treaty. Assume that there is an income tax treaty in force between the United States and

Denmark and that the treaty is identical to the 2006 U.S. Model Income Tax Treaty. Will the treaty help Anne?

TASK #2

Advise Anne as to how to best minimize (or avoid) being subject to tax in the United States in 2010.

TASK #3

Examine Forms 8833 and 8233. Must Anne complete either one or both of these if she wishes to claim treaty benefits?

REFERENCES — AVAILABLE IN ONLINE MATERIALS

IRC §§ 7701(a)(30), 7701(b), 7852(d), 894(a), 6114
Treas. Reg. §§ 301.7701(b)-2, -8; 301.6114-1
2006 United States Model Income Tax Treaty
IRS Publication 901, U.S. Tax Treaties
IRS Publication 519, U.S. Tax Guide for Aliens
IRS Form 8833, Treaty-Based Return Position Disclosure
IRS Form 8233, Exemption from Withholding on Compensation
IRS Form 8840, Closer Connection Exception Statement for Aliens
IRS Form 1040NR, U.S. Nonresident Alien Income Tax Return

A SELF STUDY ASSESSMENT IS AVAILABLE IN THE ONLINE MATERIALS